# FIND YOUR DIVINE RHYTHM

## A CREATIVE'S SUCCESS FORMULA



**DORI STAEHLE, MBA**

Dori Staehle

# Table of Contents

Dori Staehle

**What others are saying about this book:**

"Talented Dori Staehle is a first-class artist and quite a good writer. She thinks like an artist, feels like an artist and acts like an artist. She has managed to transform grim pain into productive outlets. Her insight based on setbacks and struggle allows her to speak courageously and honestly to the next generation of free spirits who don't want to settle. "Find Your Divine Rhythm: A Creative's Success" allows readers a peek into a private world without the stunning easy successes so they can gain and grow from them. Highly readable."
– Michael Ray Smith, Professor of Journalism, Palm Beach Atlantic University, author of *Seven Days to a Byline That Pays* (release date of August 3 from Lighthouse Publishing).

"All I can say is, WOW! What a wonderful journey you will go on reading this book. I enjoyed Dori's tales of injury, calling by God, and experiencing new victory in her life. As a fellow music lover, I really appreciated the impact music has on Dori's life. It does on my life as well. Very motivating." – Joseph Novara, speaker and best-selling author *of Intentional Networking: Your Guide to Word of Mouth Marketing Greatness.*

" Fantastic Book!!! I read through it twice! I'll be reading it again and again to stay motivated. At 50something, I decided to quit my job and chase my dream: Music. This book is a wealth of information not only for the creative musician, but for anyone starting something new...whether a business, a career, or a whole new life. Author, musician, speaker, teacher, film maker, entrepreneur, new career, new direction, this book is for you. You'll read it again and again and again. Thanks, Dori for such a great resource at the tip of my fingers!"
– Robyn Frateschi, singer and recording artist

"*Find Your Divine Rhythm* unites a passion for doing what you love with practical and meaningful suggestions on how to succeed in doing it. I love Dori's enthusiasm and practical advice and thoroughly enjoyed this book. Chapter 6, 'Creating Momentum and Staying Power,' was particularly inspiring to me as I recognize that it's one thing to start to do what you love and another to do it in such a way that you create a lasting career of it. I highly recommend this to anyone who doesn't fit the norm - and is happy about that - and wants to start, or start over, living and working to the beat of their own drum."
- William Dickinson, massage therapist

FIND YOUR DIVINE RHYTHM: A Creative's Success Formula



The publisher has strived to be as accurate and complete as possible in the creation of this book.

This book is not intended for use as a source of legal, business, accounting, medical, psychiatric, or financial advice. All readers are advised to seek services of competent professionals in these fields.

In practical advice books, as in anything else in life, there are no guarantees of income made. The suggestions within this book are based on the author's experience. Individual results may vary.

While all attempts have been made to verify information provided for this publication, the publisher assumes no responsibility for errors, omissions, or contrary interpretation of the subject matter herein. Any perceived slights of specific persons, peoples, or organizations are unintended.

# *A Special Bonus from Dori*

This book is the start of your journey to understanding what makes you unique, what has been tripping you up, and how you can use your gifts and talents to succeed. I'm sharing my story and plenty of tips to help you move forward and create a solid income.

It took me several years to bounce back and find my rhythm. It also took quite a lot of soul-searching and conversations with God. These conversations became daily journal entries. I am sharing some of these entries in the form of a 30-day affirmations journal which is yours free! It will help you stay focused and encouraged and see the big picture. You can print out a page a day or leave it on your computer.

You can download your copy here:
http://www.rockthenextstage.com/divine-rhythm-journal

*Get ready to rock!*

*Dori*

*Dedication*

This book is dedicated to all the creative, talented, and gifted individuals out there, including all the bands and solo artists I've booked and managed over the years.

It's also dedicated to my sisters, Diane and Carol, my daughter Niki, and my son Evan who taught me that it's ok to march to the beat of a different drummer.

Dori Staehle

# Acknowledgments

I'd like to thank my husband Mark for his constant love and support and for putting up for me while I wrote this book! His quiet demeanor and even keel have kept me going when things felt like they were falling apart. Of course, I owe my life and this book to my Creator and Divine Healer.

Heartfelt thanks also go out to those who pushed me to stay strong and to claim my gifts and talents, and helped me move forward. This includes my good friend and music buddy William Simkiss, the highly intuitive dynamo Sheyenne Kreamer, the amazingly spiritual and encouraging Ericka D. Jackson, the ever-inspiring Leslie Flowers and Diana Needham who helped me finish the book process, and the Southern powerhouse Barnsley Brown who wouldn't let me give up, even when I wanted to. Thanks to all for checking up on me and being there for me!

Thanks also to Annette Rhodes and Gabrielle McKeithen and Dr. Baric and Debby at the Chiropractic Nutrition Center for their help and support and for helping me reclaim my health and my life.

I also need to give a shout out to my "supporting cast". These are people who probably don't realize that what they said and did mattered. This includes Jim Yadon, Wendy Kraft, Tim Currin, Dave Seymour, Joe Novara, Karen Sullivan, Blake Matthews, Jason Damico, Kevin Angier, and Tommy Niemann. Thanks also to Sheila E who inspired me to drum and to share my story and Robyn Frateschi and Katrina Pfankuch for their inspiration and support.

Finally, I'd like to thank my Mavenzmind sisters and the lovely ladies in TAG Christian Business Women's Network, Marilyn Shannon and the women in Women's Power Networking, the ladies at Grace Church, as well as all the talented and amazing people I've had the pleasure of coaching and working with! *You rock!!*

# Preface

*If a man does not keep pace with his companions, perhaps it is because he hears a different drummer. Let him step to the music which he hears, however measured or far away.*
*~ Henry David Thoreau*

Why do so many bright, creative, and talented people feel stuck and unsure about their direction?  Why do we have difficulty claiming our gifts and earning what we're worth? What happened to make us doubt our abilities and question our purpose? Why do we often sabotage ourselves and can't seem to get ahead?

I've worked with extremely bright, creative, and talented teens and adults for close to 20 years. These questions have puzzled me for some time. I felt we need to get to the root cause of all this, in order to stop the cycle of underachievement and under-earning. I have helped many creatives gain clarity and confidence, rediscover their gifts, and create an income doing what they love. Some were struggling with anxiety, depression, low self-esteem, and ADHD issues.

However, I never would have predicted that I would also stumble and fall and that it would take three years to get back on my feet and figure out how the heck to move forward! It was a long, hard journey but in the end, I was able to reconnect with my true passion, get unstuck, and heal. I was also able to create a business that rocks and a life that I love. Life's short! Isn't it time to finally use your gifts and talents to create a solid income?

**Your natural rhythm**

We all have our own natural rhythm, which forms our spiritual DNA. You were given your gifts and talents for a reason. There is a purpose and a mission that was intended specifically for you.

Since you're reading this right now, my guess is that you are still wondering what that purpose and mission is. You may not even know what your talents and gifts are. So, let me ask you a few questions:

- ❖ **Are you ready to take your creativity, your life, and your purpose to the next stage? Are you in the mid-season of life and feeling stuck or confused about your direction?**

❖ **Have you had a change in circumstances and know it's time for a change?**

❖ **Are ADHD symptoms preventing you from focusing and finishing things? Do you need clarity, direction, and a solid game plan?**

❖ **Do you want to use your talents to create a business or a non-profit but don't know where to start? Or did you start a creative business but it just isn't taking off?**

❖ **Are you feeling pulled to do something else but are worried that it's not "practical" or you're not sure if this is what God or the Universe intended for you?**

❖ **Are you super-bright and super-talented and are wondering: a) Why you're not as successful as you could be and b) When is it your turn to make your mark on the world?!**

**If so, this book is for you!**

**Who this book is not for:**

- ❖ Hobbyists: People who just want to dabble in a creative endeavor on the side and aren't interested in creating an income from it.
- ❖ Job seekers: People who are seeking job hunting and resume writing tips.
- ❖ People who aren't open to possibilities and different ways to succeed.
- ❖ Those who aren't willing to do the work to help them move forward.

**What you can hope to get out of this book:**

- ❖ Clarity derived from brainstorming possibilities for this stage of your life.
- ❖ Aha! Moments when you see what's really tripping you up.
- ❖ Possibilities for converting your passions into full-time income.
- ❖ Confidence that you can move ahead with your dreams.
- ❖ Inspiring stories, tips, and action steps from someone who rose from the ashes and started a creative business with next to nothing.

## Why I wrote this book and how to use it

If you've taken time off to raise your kids, gotten laid off, or are in a job that you hate, you may not realize your gifts and your options. I wrote this book to provide a roadmap to help gifted, creative, and talented types navigate their way around their doubts and fears, so that they can clear a path to their purpose and to profits.

After being knocked down and losing nearly everything, it was hard for me to start over – especially since I was over 50! I wasted a good deal of time and money trying to figure out why what I was doing wasn't working. It wasn't until I finally realized that I couldn't do this on my own and asked God for help that healing and clarity began to appear. You may not believe all that transpired but I assure you that it was amazing and miraculous.

I was told I need to share my story with other creative types to get them unstuck as well. Although I resisted at first, I realized that I was given my story for a reason - and so were you. It's time to find out what that is so that you can stop struggling and rise up and rock your next stage!

You can read through this book alone, or as part of one of my workshops, retreats, or coaching programs. Info (and a special bonus!) will be at the end of this book. There are many exercises throughout which are labeled *Take 5!* Taking time to read and do these exercises will help with clarity. I've also added some "tweetable" quotes with the hashtag #findyourdivinerhythm. Feel free to tweet these or just reflect on them a bit.

Understanding your unique rhythm is the key to helping you move forward. And so our journey begins....

# *Introduction*

Ever since I was little, I have been intrigued by, and addicted to, rhythm. I heard beats in my head constantly! I would tap out beats with anything I could get my hands on - pencils, silverware, chopsticks, or whatever I found lying around. If I didn't have anything immediately at my disposal, I would just tap out beats with my feet under the table. I had more energy than I knew what to do with!

While other little kids were watching cartoons on Saturday mornings, I was watching old movies and studying the dance moves of Gene Kelly, Fred Astaire, Ginger Rodgers, and the great tapper, Ann Miller. I was hooked!

## From adversity comes creativity

Studies have shown that creativity often stems from a difficult or traumatic childhood. If that's the case, then I guess I qualify. Let's just say my family put the *fun* in dysfunction. We were the talk of the neighborhood. But no one wanted to get involved.

My Mom was an alcoholic who frequented the neighborhood bars during the day. I was left home alone since age 3 or 4 and often went without food. My memories of my Mom were either seeing her passed out on the couch, or flying into angry and violent rages. It was my older sister who was on the receiving end of these fits, which I unfortunately observed. I quickly learned that if you kept your mouth shut, you didn't get hit. I became so quiet that you could barely hear me. In fact, I often mumbled – especially around adults.

One morning, we woke up and discovered that our Mom packed up during the night and took off. There was no note or explanation. I was not quite five. That's when I became a dancer. And that's when my Dad became a single parent of three young girls. He had no idea of all the abuse and neglect that was taking place when he was at work and the fact that we were practically raising ourselves. Actually, my sister Diane was the one who raised me. I wished I could have prevented our family from falling apart. I was the mediator. But it wasn't enough.

Music became a big part of my life and a great refuge from the chaos all around me. I made it to lead dancer status and was always placed in the front row so that all the other dancers could follow. I would frequently daydream in school and choreograph dance numbers in my head.

I eventually began taking singing lessons and I learned how to play the guitar. My guitar was great for writing and playing songs but it didn't really excite me. I decided it was time to ask for the instrument that I really wanted to play: drums.

## Little drummer girl

My Dad said that drums would be too noisy. We lived in a two-family house, so he had a point there. Girls also didn't play drums. I became fascinated with drum solos, however, and would regularly listen to drummers like Ginger Baker (from Cream), Buddy Rich, and other rock and jazz artists that were on the records we had at home. I decided I wanted to become the first female drummer. Apparently, that title was already taken by Viola Smith thirty years earlier. She was followed by Karen Carpenter and many others.

My Dad was a former musician and singer who played with some of the jazz greats in New York City and also played weddings. After he married my Mom, he went into advertising. When he was away at his day job, I would experiment on the bongos, the conga drum, the maracas, and other instruments that my Dad had hanging around.

My connection with drums can't be put into words. My beats expressed my feelings and expressed my story. It was also my secret. No one in the family knew I played. Music and art, as my Dad explained, just weren't practical. When I would watch a band play, I was always fixated on the drums. In my head and in my heart, I was playing.

Things got really chaotic after my Dad remarried. My sisters had moved out and I was the only remaining memory of a failed marriage and the woman who walked out. Money issues were pervasive. I was on the receiving end of quite a bit of verbal and emotional abuse, from both my Dad and my stepmother. By this point, I had a half-sister and half-brother, whom I often took care of. I tried to be the perfect daughter but it wasn't enough.

At age 16, I packed up and left home. I remember feeling very angry, hurt, and confused. As I was leaving, I heard a very quiet voice whisper "Don't give up. I have plans for you." That was the first time I heard God's voice. It wouldn't be the last.

I stayed with a friend and her family and later moved home for a few months before graduation. As I was heading off to college, my Dad said "Have a nice life." And that was it. I was out of his life and out of the way. I left him, and the drums, behind.

Finally, at age 47, with the beats in my head and a whole lot of guts, I auditioned for a rockin' church band. I've been playing percussion with them for about eight years and have never had a single lesson. I also discovered a way to use drums to help people gain clarity and confidence so they can find what makes their heart sing and create a business doing what they love. Drums can also help people heal. I know this because I did all of this myself.

I rose up from some major setbacks and started a creative business with only $40 in the bank. And it started with three little words…..

24

**Chapter 1**

**Hearing the Music: When You Need a Plan B**

"Dori! Look out!" It was the voice of my co-worker. I was working in sales and marketing and we were outside at a weekend-long event with about 200 clients. I saw my co-worker zip past me in a golf cart. He was doing a tour with three beautiful young blondes, so I decided to run up to him and crack a joke. "Tough gig!" I laughed. He was now in the distance and saw it coming. I, however, did not.

As I looked to my left, I suddenly saw the approaching danger. A young man was flying through the crowd on a speeding bicycle and was headed right for me! I didn't have time to get out of the way. I heard a voice in my head say "Lean back" and then bam! I got hit on my left side with about as much force as a football tackle, except I wasn't wearing any padding.

My torso quickly snapped forward as the handlebars smashed

into my left arm. I then got slammed to the right, as the massive G-force overpowered my 111- pound frame. My body then careened forward. I saw the bricks of the pavement quickly approaching and I told myself "Pull up! Pull up! Pull up!" I used every muscle in my body to try to remain upright but I kept falling.

My former runner instincts kicked in and I threw my right shoulder forward to brace for impact. This technique prevents your head from hitting the pavement, in the event of a fall. Miraculously, the only thing that made contact with the ground was my right hand. I pushed off the pavement with my hand and stood back up. I then searched for my backpack which got tossed over my head and landed several yards to my left. I remember feeling extremely angry and embarrassed. I was also thankful I wasn't wearing a dress that day!

I jumped up, made the touchdown sign to the crowd, and said "I'm good!" At least, I thought I was. When the bicyclist came back to ask me if I was ok, I started asking him ridiculous questions like "Are you in a band?" I had no idea that this was an indication that I was in shock. No one came to see if I was ok. No one called security. No one filled out an accident report and no one got the young man's name. In three seconds, he was gone. I then corralled everyone because we needed to head inside for a presentation.

## The Perfect Storm

It happened in all of 30 seconds but my life was forever altered. Little did I know that this accident would cause multiple injuries and trigger a rare disease; it would also cause me to have to quit my job and let go of two businesses I spent nearly 20 years developing. My life and my bank account began their descent and I slowly slipped down the rabbit hole. Things were very dark indeed. The good news, as you'll soon see, is that the accident was also a blessing.

I don't think anyone realized that I was seriously injured, including me. At first, I was just having pain in my lower back, left knee, left ankle, and right hip. Then, my right shoulder began hurting and my right arm began going numb. Back spasms became so constant I just got used to them, along with the headaches. My husband Mark got used to me sleeping on the couch.

When my feet began going numb and I couldn't move my legs, I knew that something was seriously wrong. Feeling was restored but then replaced by shooting tailbone pain. Despite applying frequent ice packs during the day, I still had two visible masses on my back. I was sent to several doctors and physical therapists. My concerns were dismissed. Critical mistakes were made regarding my treatment which created the perfect storm.

Despite the fact that I was only getting about three hours of sleep every night, I continued to go to work. Caffeine became my friend. Stairs became my enemy. One of my co-workers joked that maybe we should order one of those electric wheelchairs that go up steps. Others suggested that I wear a reflector vest outside so that people can see me or put rocks in my pocket so I won't blow away. Sure, let's make fun of the skinny chick! Ok, so these jokes were pretty funny.

With our busy season approaching, I knew there was no way I'd be able to keep up and do all the traveling and other physical demands that my job required. Months had gone by and I was still in pain. So, I handed in my resignation. I provided one month's notice so that I could train my replacement. I learned that wouldn't be necessary. My position was being eliminated. I was stunned. I was the only one who had experience with my very specific target market and created special marketing materials and website pages. Like me, all of that would soon be gone.

Two weeks later, I packed up my belongings, while my co-workers fought over my comfy office chair. It wasn't even cold yet! There was no going away party and no fanfare. I held back the tears, handed over the keys to the company car, and slipped out the back door. A friend picked me up, took me out to lunch, and drove me home. It was September of 2011, nearly three months after the accident.

I thought I'd be back to normal in two to three weeks and I'd just return to running my two businesses from home. Business #1 involved tutoring, SAT prep, ADHD coaching, educational consulting, and homeschooling support. Business #2 involved concert booking and promotion for young, local bands and solo artists. I also managed a few bands as well. I had no idea that it would take three years to recover and everything would be turned upside down. After all, I was hit by a 10-speed, not a car or a forklift. Who in the world gets run over by a bicycle?!

I wondered how God could let this happen. Then, I met with a bass player friend for coffee. Jim asked: "Did it ever occur to you that maybe God needed you to be somewhere else?" No, actually, it hadn't. The signs were there but I ignored them, I guess. That was one heck of a way to get my attention!

Another friend who is a music teacher extraordinaire and a former pastor reminded me of what *didn't* happen and how God intervened. I have a really good visual memory, which I used to recreate the scene for him. It was a scene that I had replayed over and over in my mind. William pointed out all the things that my body could have hit but missed, including the refreshment table, a cement pole with a map on it, several trees, and about 50 people to my right. The bicyclist missed everyone else, including the two little girls who were right near me. I then realized I blocked the hit. I kept thinking that I was just in the wrong place at the wrong time.

"Maybe you were in the **right** place at the **right** time. God knew what he was doing," William laughed.

Has life ever thrown you a curveball? Have you ever been zipping along just fine and then wham! Something comes at you completely out of left field. What was your "bicycle"? What knocked you for a loop? Have you ever wondered "Why me?!" All I can say is: *Stuff happens*. I've been through the wringer so many times that I know the adage is true: "It's always darkest before the dawn."

## *Take 5!*

Has something thrown you for a loop? Re-frame it and see the blessing in the lesson. Take some time to jot your thoughts down on a pad or in your journal: "If _________ didn't happen, then I wouldn't have….."

## The face of change

I'm told I have something called *The Resiliency Factor* because I always bounce back. I've overcome a difficult childhood, anorexia, endometriosis, infertility, six layoffs (five for my husband and one for me), and many moves. Mark and I have lived in five states and 11 houses. Sometimes the moves were due to corporate relocations. Others were because we could no longer afford our mortgage. There were times when we shopped at the food bank with two little kids in tow and relied on our church to help us pay the bills. I also experienced a breast cancer scare at age 40.

After the accident, I decided that I just needed to press on and continued to attend networking events and do guest speaking gigs. No one knew that I was wearing either Ace® bandages or Icy Hot Patches® under my clothes to help ease the pain. It became part of my routine. I'm a tough cookie. What I used to tell my bands was "Unless you're dying, the show must go on."

A chiropractor asked me what I was using to help deal with the pain. I told him: "Denial. And red wine." I told him I had been given pain relievers and muscle relaxers but they made me even dizzier and violently ill. I only took them once. I'm not a big fan of traditional medicine. It took months to get approval for chiropractic visits. I was thankful that I was still covered under worker's compensation, but dealing with the insurance company was a nightmare. Chiropractic treatments felt good temporarily but I kept slipping out of alignment shortly after my visits.

The insurance company offered to send me to other doctors and that's when my trip to Wonderland began. The constant arguing with the insurance company and the doctors created additional stress and really wore me down. This was nothing short of bullying and harassment. No one is on your side when you're injured at work, as I discovered. Yes, I understand that some people fake injuries. However, this patient was definitely not faking! I know when something is wrong. Disagreeing with a doctor is apparently not allowed, even if you've spent 20 years doing medical research. I had spent years fighting for my young clients and watching their backs. I wished I had someone to watch mine.

A year after the accident, I took it upon myself to find a really good chiropractor who was known for looking at the whole picture. This chiropractor's X-rays revealed that I had whiplash, multiple sprains and tears, and a possible concussion. This would explain the pain levels and my new symptom: memory issues. I kept forgetting words for common things. I also sometimes mixed up words and would say *brain* instead of *music*, for example. As a guest speaker and teacher, this was not good! He was amazed that I had been to so many physicians and no one caught any of this. So was I. Actually, *amazed* wasn't how I felt; ***extremely ticked off*** was more like it.

Dramatic improvements were seen because of the chiropractic treatments and I was doing great! I decided I could increase my activity. In addition to teaching SAT prep classes, I began teaching career development and entrepreneurship classes at the local community college, a women's homeless shelter, and other non-profits. The classes at the shelter really touched my heart and uncovered gifts I didn't know I had.

Increased activity created increased pain and new symptoms. I also began having trouble walking, had shooting pain in my tailbone, hip, and my legs, and I was having dizzy spells. Now, I was getting really scared. I knew something was wrong but I didn't know what. Neither did my chiropractor. Two years had passed since the accident. I wrote in my journal and prayed to God. I wondered when this nightmare would end.

## Shifting sands

Life as I knew it completely changed as I had to adjust to being able to do less and less. I also had to adjust how I walked and moved. For the first time in my life, I felt old. As someone who is used to being very active and independent, it was extremely difficult asking for help. I finally had to ask Mark to take over most of the household chores and grocery shopping. These were activities that I had done for the 30+ years of our married life. Mark never really talked about it but I sensed that he was very worried. My life, and our relationship, just wasn't the same.

Before the accident, I swam 26 laps (52 pool lengths) in 30 minutes. I worked a full-time job, which included doing walking tours and traveling throughout several states to do special events and speaking gigs for my company. I often worked nights and weekends. In addition, I continued to run my music business and booked three to four large concerts a month, featuring between three and five bands. In addition to booking and promotion, I acted as the emcee and stage manager. Sometimes I organized huge Battle of the Bands events. I was the only promoter who did all this solo – and it was a blast!

In addition, I taught SAT Boot Camps, which spanned four hours on Saturday afternoons. I taught about four or five of these per year. They weren't as exciting as the concerts but they paid extremely well. I also played in the church band twice a month, which meant 2 practices and 4 services, I volunteered with the youth group, and I went on mission trips to France with the band for two weeks each summer.
After the accident, I realized I couldn't keep up that pace. Actually, my body and brain didn't seem to be operating at the same level. I had to keep reminding myself that I was once smart.

Yes, I quit the corporate world to stay home to raise our kids but I wasn't your typical stay-at-home Mom. I started my two creative businesses because of our kids. They were my first clients.

The businesses grew as I received requests to help others and I became an accidental entrepreneur. Entrepreneurship became part of my lifestyle, along with homeschooling. We homeschooled at our kids' request and continued through high school. I also booked and managed several of their bands.

Many people had no idea what type of work I did. They just thought I tutored once in a while from my home and many thought that I was a volunteer with a school's marching band program. "No! I book rock bands!" I would tell them. They didn't seem to get it, apparently. These people didn't go to clubs and weren't aware of the local music scene or the monthly Teen Band Nights I created with the local park and recreation departments.

In fact, a bank teller looked at a check I was about to deposit from one of these music events and she said "Hmm,...*Next Stage Entertainment*. Do you teach drama classes?" I had to stifle a laugh and I said "No, I book rock bands. Sometimes there's drama. Depends on the day."

I've helped hundreds of bands take their talent to the next stage. Once they were ready and their skills were solid, I booked them to open for national acts and for well-paying festival gigs. Several Teen Band Night graduates got signed and began touring. I can say I knew them when. Working with so many bands and solo artists helped me gain valuable experience that I would later use in my coaching business. Even though these guys drove me nuts sometimes, I loved doing those shows. I was very happy and I felt like I was making a difference.

**Searching for meaning – and a job!**

Although my intent was to grow my two businesses, the insurance company expected me to find a *regular* job and report back to them every month. Apparently, entrepreneurship didn't count. I continuously applied for jobs in education, sales, and the music industry and did a significant amount of networking to no avail. Apparently, I was overqualified for many of the positions that were available. I was also told my resume made me look "too smart".

So, I not only dumbed down my resume, I also deleted any experience that was more than 15 years old. There went all my corporate experience in international banking and financial sales, including the impressive job on Wall Street and the one at the French Bank in Rockefeller Plaza.

That would avoid age discrimination and get my foot in the door, or so I thought. I had a great LinkedIn photo and profile and was active on social media. I applied for loads of jobs. But I didn't get a single interview.

I felt like I had lost my purpose and my identity. Our kids were grown and gone, I had no job, my businesses were hanging by a thread, and my body was in constant pain. I was getting some consulting and tutoring gigs and taught some classes but these were very short-term in nature. I also had guest speaking gigs but these were mostly unpaid. I still had a few concerts on the books as well. I had to really suck it up to get through all of this, since my pain levels were through the roof, especially in my tailbone.

The fact remained that there was no way that I could do a regular job. I was now 54 and possibly disabled. None of this screamed "great hiring potential". I realized that I needed to switch to an automatic vehicle to keep my pain levels down, so I said goodbye to my little car with the stick shift. I also realized that entrepreneurship was my only option.

**The turning point**

There comes a point when you just get sick and tired of being sick and tired. I didn't want to play games. I wanted answers. I decided to ask the insurance company for something that might solve this medical mystery: MRI scans. They reluctantly agreed. It had been three years since the accident. Yes, this should have been done right away.

When I saw my MRI films, I noticed there were cysts all over my spine. The MRI notes indicated these were called *Tarlov cysts*. When Tarlov cysts appear with pain symptoms, it's an indication of a rare degenerative neurological condition called *Tarlov Cyst Disease*. As I checked different websites, words kept popping up like *rare disease, can be triggered by a trauma such as an accident, extremely painful,* and *no cure.* The words hit me like a ton of bricks.

"No!!" I screamed and cried. "This is what I get?! This is what I get for devoting my entire life to helping people? This is what

I get for wishing I had a better story than being hit by a bicycle?!"

I researched my options but wasn't very pleased with what I found. Surgery wasn't without risks and complications and there were no guarantees. Even if they could remove the cysts safely, there was a strong chance that they could grow back. There are only three neurosurgeons in the U.S. who are familiar with the disorder. The cost of the surgery plus airfare and expenses was outrageous.

After a lot of meditation, prayer, journaling, and listening to inspirational music, I had an idea. It occurred to me that I could work completely from home and work with clients online. That option seemed very isolating and didn't seem like much fun though. I also knew that, given my pain levels, I'd only be able to work a few hours a day. So, I made a deal with God. I asked Him to give me a way to heal myself and also to heal others. The message I got was "Look around. I already did."

As I looked around, I saw all my drums. I have nine African drums, two sets of bongos, a set of congas drums, several flat drums and a ton of percussion instruments like shakers, tambourines, etc. I had originally purchased some of these instruments to help kids beat ADHD symptoms. Drumming was the last piece of the puzzle in a theory I created called *The Gifted/ADHD Connection*. This theory was based on nearly 20 years of research and case studies (More on that later.).

This is why I had signed on for training in drum therapy and therapeutic drumming with the *Drums and Disabilities (DAD) Program* and *Health Rhythms*. I had forgotten about the healing properties of the drums and why they are used in hospitals with cancer patients and others. I then realized that drum healing could be an integral part of my work as well.

As I mentioned, I am self-taught in drumming but it's been part of my DNA for as long as I can remember. When I auditioned for the church band back in 2006, my husband and son were shocked. That's not something that a 47-year old woman generally does.

"You signed up to audition?! You haven't even had any lessons!" they exclaimed.

I figured "What the heck?" I thought that if I were really awful, the worship team leader would tell me "Don't call us, we'll call you." But he didn't. He said "See you Sunday."

With the exception of some time off after the accident, I've been playing with them ever since. I can now play all types of music including rock, pop, jazz, funk, R &B, and contemporary Christian.

When I'm with the band, I stand and play the bongos and congas, and every type of percussion instrument imaginable. I have a lot of energy and I dance and move when I play. I tell people I'm like Sheila E - without the stilettos. The church band includes professional musicians and we play tunes from artists you wouldn't expect like U2 and Van Halen. If it fits the theme and it's clean, we play it. When I'm playing I can feel the presence of the Holy Spirit, especially on the Christian tunes. It's so powerful; it almost brings me to tears.

After I received the message from God, I began sitting and drumming 15-30 minutes a day at home, mainly using an African drum called a Djembe (pronounced "jem-bay"), which has the best healing properties. I envisioned a beam of light coming down from heaven and entering my body through the top of my head. I visualized my cells being repaired and the cysts going away.

During this time, I received calls from three women I hadn't heard from in a while. They wanted to check on me and they prayed for me over the phone. One was the amazing coach, healer, evangelist, and preacher Ericka Jackson. Another introduced me to essential oils and Kombucha tea to help with the swelling and to boost my immune system. Within two weeks of my conversation with God, I was healed. No more back pain. No dizziness. No balance issues. Flexibility and range of motion were greatly improved. Numbness was gone. No more brain fog.

I had been having a dream of a graceful dancer on a beach on and off for about a year. I never considered that it could be me in the dream. After all, before I made my deal with God, I could barely move. My body felt so good afterwards though, I thought I'd try some ballet moves.

I stood next to my desk, stretched out my right leg and left arm, and did a perfect arabesque! No pain and I could balance! Not only have I been given the gift of Divine Rhythm, I was healed by the Divine Healer. The dream returned but now there was someone walking next to me on the beach. He turned to me and held my face in his hands. It was Jesus. I cried and knew I was going to be ok.

It was June of 2014, almost exactly three years since the accident, and I was finally free! I was able to return to swimming laps and many other activities that had been put on hold. What is most interesting is that there were also no more trips to *the dark side of the moon.* I'm not only referencing the Pink Floyd tune but also that place where you're so despondent that you actually think of checking out. This feeling came over me several times and I had to hold on and fight.  I had to call in heavenly reinforcements to push through the waves of despair. I didn't tell anyone, which was a mistake. I didn't want anyone to know that the person who always encouraged others was hurting. I also didn't want to hurt my family by doing something stupid.

So, I decided to stick around. The following six words confirmed my decision: "You're going to be a Grandma!" Our son and his wife were expecting. I now have an adorable grandson. And he has a rockin' and healthy Grandma!

## *Take 5!*

Did you notice the lack of family support on my decision to audition for the band? How about all those doctors who totally missed what was really going on? How many naysayers are in your life? What are the false assumptions and negative thoughts that they have planted in your head?  Write those down in a notepad. When you're done, make a big X and cross them out! You don't need those thoughts anymore!

**It's time to hit the refresh button and start over! #findyourdivinerhythm**

**Starting Over**

This is not to say that starting over was easy. There were plenty of times when I felt like I was just banging my head against the wall. I continued to attend networking events to meet other business owners and potential clients. They all seemed so successful, which made it even harder for me to smile and blend in. But I did it. I often attended three to five of these events per week.

I will share more suggestions for getting unstuck in the next chapters. One thing that I do know is that it took me longer to bounce back than I thought, especially emotionally. This took more work than I ever imagined. If you're struggling right now, here are some tips that might help:

1) **Keep the faith!** You will get through this! Keep praying, read your Bible or other spiritual and inspirational books. Try journaling and listening to music.

2) **Count your blessings**! My accident scenario could have been so much worse. I was glad to be alive and that no one else got hurt. My family doctor informed me that if the handlebars hit my chest at that speed instead of my arm, I would have died instantly. I now know why God wanted me to lean back!

3) **Get physical!** Swim, bike, run, go for a walk, shoot some hoops, or do whatever physical activity works for you. It not only helps you burn calories, it increases those *feel good endorphins*.  In addition to swimming three or four times a week, I do daily strengthening exercises to help with my core muscles.

4) **Ask for help**! Don't suffer in silence! Let people know what you need. Don't sabotage yourself and try to self-medicate with drugs or alcohol. Reach

out to a friend, relative or pastor, and God. You are not alone!

5) **Listen to see if you're making excuses.** How often do you say that you can't do things or tell your sob story? Reframe your situation and try to see the possibilities.

6) **Find what brings you joy!** I put together a bucket list and realized that just about everything on there was fun. I was spending so much time trying to make money and going in circles that I wasn't having any fun! I asked myself, what do I really love to do? Play drums, encourage people, and help them use their gifts and talents.

So, with $40 to my name and well past 50 years old, I started a new business called *Rock the Next Stage*. I purchased 3 domain names (.com, .net., and .biz) and set up a free website. I didn't want to just move onto the next stage, I wanted to rock it!

After I went for the drum therapy and therapeutic drumming training, I began to think: What if I really could just "bang on dee drum all day"? What if I made drumming a big part of *Rock the Next Stage*? How cool would that be?!! It still seemed too far-fetched. Dropping my other businesses to drum, including the highly lucrative SAT prep classes? I made every excuse in the book from "It's not practical!" to "What will people think?"

Yes, all the voices from my past, from my Dad to guidance counselors, were coming back to haunt me. Eventually, I dropped my other businesses and took the leap to *Rock the Next Stage*.

**Gearing up**

I began to remember all that enthusiasm I had when I went for my training and how I got my drums. I found out about the *Health Rhythms* program from a local drum circle facilitator. He told me that there was a training program taking place in New Jersey and that they offered scholarships.

I applied for a scholarship, got it, and hopped on a plane! I got a great deal on airfare and split the cost of the hotel and the rental car with a friend who decided to come with me. Unfortunately, I couldn't afford to purchase any drums from the vendors that weekend but I did a makeshift crowdfunding campaign and raised some money when I got back. If you're not familiar with crowdfunding, that is an online fundraising campaign. You can target friends and family and even strangers.

My bands used to use crowdfunding campaigns all the time to raise money for their CD projects. I didn't want to pay the fee for services like *Kickstarter* or *Indie Gogo*, so I tried to do it myself. I did an email campaign and got $0 donations. I just did an email. No video. Yes, I mentioned that I wanted to start a drumming program for kids with ADHD and other special needs.

No one cared, or so I thought. I eventually received funds from three individuals and was able to purchase six African drums. I paid for the percussion gear plus two additional drums on my own. A local drum shop gave me a great discount on all eight drums. In addition to selling instruments and teaching drum lessons, they also train young musicians and put them in bands. I've booked some of these talented bands. Like they say, what goes around comes around. I pay it forward by sending them customers.

**Tip:** If you're going to do a crowdfunding campaign, use a service like *Kickstarter, Indie Gogo*, or *Go Fund Me*. Make sure you do a halfway decent video, explain what you're raising the money for, and what contributors will get for their donations. It helps if you offer perks for different levels of contribution. You don't need fancy equipment for your video. You can use your phone or your laptop. I'd recommend a program like *Movie Maker* or *i-Movie*, depending on your computer, which are free. There is also a program called *Animoto.* Don't just use email. Use social media as well. Frequently.

**Note:** Crowdfunding campaigns are great if you have a good cause or you have something to give your contributors in exchange for their donation. I personally don't think it's right to ask for money for things like a new computer or printer for your home office, for example. Yes, I've seen people do that.

**Making ends meet**

If you've been thrown for a loop and the funds are running out, there are many ways to make money and yes, they're legitimate. First, I sold some high-ticket items that I no longer needed such as sound equipment and some jewelry. I also bartered for services and I found some contract work. If you write, consult, or do web or graphic design, you might want to check out *Freelancer* (www.freelancer.com) or *Elance* (www.elance.com). Tutoring is another good source of income, if you have an area of expertise and you're good with kids.

You could also hold garage sales, shop at thrift stores, cut your own hair, do your own nails, and cut back or completely eliminate eating out. Make your own tea or coffee and skip the $4 cup of Starbucks. Cut coupons, look for specials, and cook and bake from scratch, instead of buying expensive (and unhealthy) frozen dinners or junk food. Drink water instead of soda. You'll not only save money, you'll lose weight and be healthier!

In addition, you might want to renegotiate your contract with the cable company, drop some channels, or eliminate cable altogether. I also found a very affordable cell phone plan.

**Staying positive**

There is also something to be said for positive thinking and the *Law of Attraction*. While many feel that the *Law of Attraction* is a new concept, or even New Age, it actually dates way back. It was not discovered by the writers of the book and movie, *The Secret*! Elements of this law can be traced back to biblical times, specifically to Abraham. It was also used in ancient

Greece, by Plato. Sir Isaac Newton had theories that also espoused these principles.

The premise is that *like attracts like*. If you keep telling yourself things will never work out, then they won't. If you release the thought and intention that good things are coming your way, then they will. It sounds cheesy and lame but it really helped me hold on.

There were many times when I felt like I was living the musician's credo: *Fake it till you make it!* Faking it isn't always good (for musicians or anyone, really). However, neither is wallowing in self-pity. If you can't pull yourself out of the pit, you may need to reach out and ask for help. Don't be too proud! It's better than suffering silently. Many churches offer free counseling, as do some non-profits.

Another tip would be to **get out of the house**! Go take a walk in nature or go get some exercise. Volunteer for a cause or organization. Force yourself to get together with friends and family. If you don't have people nearby, find kindred spirits on MeetUp (www.meetup.com). There are MeetUps for every possible interest, as well as professional MeetUps for networking. Sometimes you have to pay a small fee for drinks or snacks. Other times, there may be a speaker and that might be a fee as well. When things were really tight, I actually had to cash in coins just to be able to go to some of these events. I made hundreds of contacts though!

I attended a ton of workshops and signed up for online training. Much of this was free, although some I paid for. Some community colleges offer free career development classes for those who are unemployed or underemployed, so you might want to investigate this option as well. Nothing beats coaching with a coach or accountability partner, however.

**Avoid the comparison trap**! Everyone is on their own path and success happens at different times for different people.

**Stop comparing yourself to others! It's your life and your journey! #findyourdivinerhythm**

One thing that some of these coaches brought up that I had never been taught before was to ask God or the Universe for what you need and **be specific**. Yes, God already knows what you need but you need to be ready to receive. You also need to be really clear about what you want.

## *Take 5!*

Things often appear the darkest before the dawn. Can you think of any time when you were ready to give up but something amazing happened that turned things around? Maybe someone appeared to help you at just the right moment. God can clear paths for you, if you let Him.

What do you think you need to make your dream happen? Start making a list! Now, hold those things in your mind and pray about them daily. Don't be surprised if they begin to appear. Then, take action!

**Book recommendations:**

*The Gift of Change: Spiritual Guidance for Living Your Best Life*, by Marianne Williamson, ©2004, Harper Collins, pub.

*Leveraging the Universe: 7 Steps to Engaging Life's Magic*, Mike Dooley, ©2011, Atria Publishing

**Drumming info:**

Health Rhythms: www.healthrhythms.org

Drums and Disabilities (DAD) program: www.dad.org

*The Healing Power of the Drum: A Psychotherapist Explores the Healing Power of Rhythm*, by Robert Lawrence Friedman, ©2000, White Cliffs Media, pub.

Drumming page on my website:
www.rockthenextstage.com/drumming

Dori Staehle

# Chapter 2

## Tempo Issues: Why You're Missing the Beat

If you've been going in circles for a while, it's probably because there are certain underlying issues going on that you have not addressed or simply aren't aware of. Something doesn't feel quite right. It feels like your tempo is off but you're not sure why.

So, you ignore it and go about your life playing it safe because safe is easy. It also seems practical. After all, you need to pay the bills so why rock the boat? But you're still not happy and it's gnawing away at you.

Want to know the #1 reason that people don't make a change? **Fear**. They also haven't gotten in to touch with their raison d' etre or their "why".

**Hopes and dreams**

Children don't worry about the future as much as adults do.

They're too busy having fun and being kids. There are no bills to pay or bosses to answer to. If you've ever spent any time around little ones, you'd see that they have big hopes and dreams and loads of creativity and imagination.

When I thought back to my childhood dreams, I realized that the things I wanted to do involved teaching, music, and helping people. Although I never achieved my goals of dancing on Broadway or becoming a Rockette, music is still a big part of my life. I also didn't become an art or music teacher but I now teach artists and musicians (and loads of other people!) how to convert their talent into a full-time business. And I found a way to turn my fun hobby of drumming into something that brings joy and healing to people of all ages.

Let's use our imaginations for a moment. Imagine if it were possible to bend the space/time continuum. Your younger self is now standing before you. Would he or she be pleased or disappointed at your career choice or the way your life turned out? That was the premise of the movie *The Kid,* with Bruce Willis. Bruce plays an obnoxious and unhappy image consultant who is visited by his eight-year old self. Little Bruce can't believe that Big Bruce has sold out and never became a pilot. As you may have guessed, once Big Bruce re-visits his childhood dreams, his life is magically transformed.

Yes, I know what you're thinking. Life isn't a Disney movie. However, I've met many unhappy, disillusioned, and bitter adults in my life. And my advice is to remember what they loved to do as a kid – and do it! Breaking out the paints for a little while or getting that guitar out of the closet and strumming it can not only transport you back in time but it can release blockages and give you instant clarity. Listen to your inner child!

How about you? What did you enjoy doing as a kid? What did you want to be when you grew up? Do you see a pattern? Are you doing any of those things now, either directly or indirectly? Were you a rebel and did you want to change the world? What happened?

**Rebel with 100 causes**

You may be familiar with the old James Dean movie, *Rebel Without a Cause*. Well, I'm the rebel with 100 causes. It started as early as elementary school. In sixth grade, I cut a sash out of black fabric and painted a white peace sign on it. I tied it onto my left arm, right under my shoulder, as a form of silent protest of the Vietnam War.

I got marched to the principal's office. "Dori, you're so quiet! You're such a good student! How could you?! This is so unpatriotic!"

"All I know is that my sister's friends went to war. And they didn't come back. I don't think war is the answer," I replied.

They were shocked. This wasn't my first time in the principal's office. I wasn't a bad kid. I was actually very shy and didn't even talk much back then. I just didn't always speak at appropriate times. They blamed it on my upbringing and "Well, she comes from a broken home, you know."

That was the first time I stood up for something. But it wouldn't be my last. I have a problem with things that just aren't right. Medicating millions of creative, talented, and gifted kids just because Big Pharma sold our country a bill of goods isn't right. It isn't right that many of them just happen to be boys and just happen to be minorities. It isn't right that we know our public school system needs to be changed but no one wants to make the necessary changes. I even proposed a plan to a large school district that would have been so easy and cheap to implement. But they said no. In fact, my research, ideas, and advocacy efforts did not get me promoted. They got me blacklisted!

It isn't right that our educational system stifles creativity, individuality, and divergent thinking. There isn't just one way to learn and do things. Not everyone is going to be a scientist, engineer, computer programmer, or mathematician (the basic components of the nation-wide "STEM" program). It isn't right to eliminate the arts from this equation. It isn't right to discourage our future creatives. It isn't right to push college and the corporate life on everyone and never, ever mention entrepreneurship and other viable options.

I've tried to work for several other schools and colleges but it's hard when you always see things that need to be fixed. I was quickly able to see how to do things better, faster, and cheaper, and how to give the students a better experience. I discovered that having lots of ideas isn't always valued, however. In fact, it usually got me into trouble.

No matter where I went, it always seemed like I was operating at a different tempo. It seemed like everyone else was just looking at one tiny piece of the puzzle, while I was looking at the whole thing and how all the pieces fit. I like to brainstorm and I have lots of ideas. I am able to quickly go from Point A to Point F and offer multiple solutions to solve a problem. In teacher training programs, I was told I was too much of a hot shot. I've also been told that others find my ideas threatening. I was just trying to help but others don't always see it that way.

I realized that I work well **with** others but not **for** others. I found that I had to change myself too much to fit in. Once you've been burned and betrayed a few times, it really rattles you. You begin to wonder if you'll ever be able to be yourself or work for others.

**Dissonant chords**

Has that ever happened to you? Have you ever worked for a company or an organization and always felt like the odd man (or woman) out? Does speaking up get you into trouble? Do you have lots of ideas about different ways to do things? Guess what? Most rebels make great entrepreneurs. Most are also gifted.

Society doesn't like us to use that word, however, since it sounds pretentious. Many school districts feel it's politically incorrect. In fact, they'd rather give us the label ADHD (attention deficit disorder) or ODD (oppositional defiance disorder). I always say I come from a long line of artists and musicians. We're all a little odd.

Yes, everyone has gifts and talents. I firmly believe this. Everyone also has a certain degree of creativity and can use it every day, whether they are aware of it or not. This is called "Little C" creativity. I'd like to describe "Big C" creativity (Kaufman and Beghetto, 2008), since this is what highly gifted, talented, and creative people possess. It's all part and parcel of the concept known as *giftedness*; a concept that most people are not familiar with. Since I'm considered a giftedness and an ADHD expert and because this affects you, it's time for some clarification.

**Isn't everyone gifted?**

The term *gifted* has been misused for decades. Many educators feel that a student is gifted *in* something as in "Suzy is gifted in math" or "Jason is a gifted athlete". This type of reasoning is what caused school districts to focus only on language arts and math to identify gifted students. Those who had tremendous potential in other areas such as science, art, or music were completely overlooked. No one seemed to realize that that there is a complex phenomenon known as giftedness which creates unique cognitive, academic, social, emotional, and even physiological differences, as I discovered.

In fact, after the Sputnik era, funding for gifted programs was slashed to the bare bones. In many states, these programs were completely eliminated. Others offered limited programming once or twice a week for 20 or 30 minutes. Big deal! These classes were only for students who were identified by achievement tests or sometimes group IQ tests (which aren't very accurate) but not until third or fourth grade.

This not only caused millions of gifted kids to be left behind but educators weren't (and still aren't) aware that your extremely bright and creative kids don't do well on standardized tests because we tend to be right-brained. We think in pictures, not words or numbers. It takes time to convert those pictures in our heads and as a result, we stink at timed tests!

Now, some people feel that all this talk about brain dominance is nonsense and unscientific. In actuality, we use both sides of our brain. You also have to factor in hand dominance. However, there is definitely a difference in those of us who are more creative. As the following chart illustrates, the further you go on the "right-brain" continuum and the higher your IQ, the more pronounced your ADHD-type symptoms will be as well. This doesn't mean that you have the mysterious condition known as ADHD, however.

## The Left/Right-Brained Continuum

Fellow ADHD expert Jeffrey Freed has written about the mislabeling dilemma in his book, *Right-Brained Children in a Left-Brained World.* The higher people's IQs are and the further along the right-brained continuum they fall, the more pronounced the ADHD symptoms and learning issues will be – and the greater chance they have of being mislabeled.

Here's my simplified explanation of this concept:

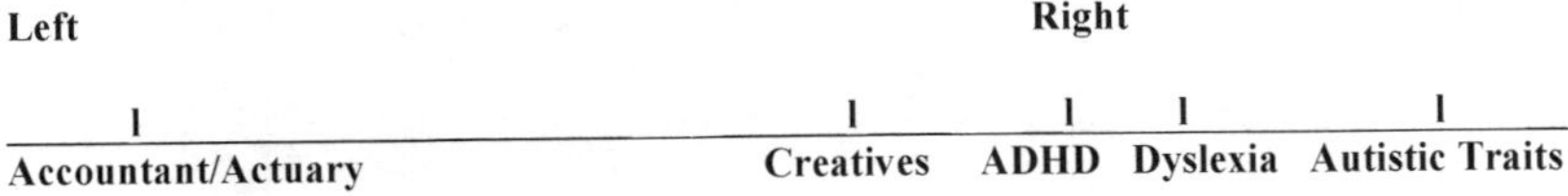


The problem is that school is a left-brained institution designed for left-brained learners. Unfortunately, 80% of gifted kids are right-brained dominant and are very visual and/or spatial. (Benbow 1986). So, if you're good in math or you're an auditory learner, you'll do well in school. If not, you're considered broken and in need of fixing and will probably be labeled ADHD, LD (learning disabled), etc. We have therefore created generations of angry, frustrated, and underachieving kids who later become confused, unfulfilled, and bitter adults. Have I hit a nerve yet?

The biggest problem is that teachers were taught that the word *gifted* meant "smart kid who gets good grades". That's the definition of a *high achiever*. There is also no such thing as *academically gifted* or *academically talented*. You cannot be *gifted* or *talented* in academics! That just means you're smart and you know how to study. Period. High achievers aren't necessarily gifted and gifted kids aren't necessarily high achievers. Unfortunately, parents and teachers put a load of expectations onto students who receive the *gifted* label.

Gifted kids don't always get good grades. Unlike the bright, high-achieving kids, they're generally not the teacher's pet and may get into trouble. They tend to act out, tune out, or drop out. It depends if they feel like playing the game or not. I spent most of junior high in detention and got mostly B's and C's (except in the subjects I liked like art and science). By the time I got to high school, I figured out how to play the game and I chose to play it.

My motivation was that I decided I wanted to graduate within the top 10% of my class, go to college, and get a full ride.

Since I was discouraged from going to college by my Dad and my guidance counselor, this was my form of rebellion. Mission accomplished – on all counts. My Dad told me that you can be creative **or** smart but you can't be both. I believed him. And I left my creativity behind.

So what is giftedness? Giftedness is a complex phenomenon which encompasses high levels of intelligence, creativity, and asynchronous development, along with heightened sensitivities (combined definition by *The Columbus Group and Linda Silverman 1991, and this author*.) Asynchronous or uneven development in a highly gifted child would be the six year-old who can do algebra but still can't tie his shoes. Many highly gifted adults can do complex tasks easily but struggle with things that others find easy. Albert Einstein, for example, didn't talk until age four and didn't read until age ten.

He could do complex mathematical equations but struggled with basic arithmetic. Einstein, like Thomas Edison and many others, was considered defective by his teachers. There is a long list of extremely bright, creative, and talented people who left school for these reasons and blossomed by learning at home (including our 2 kids!). Many were autodidacts, or self-taught. Others were taught by a parent, a tutor, or a mentor. Several in the arts had benefactors or apprenticeships. Yes, there was a day when young gifted, talented, and creative types were celebrated and supported, instead of being denigrated and medicated.

It was our daughter who first spoke up. She got tired of waiting to be challenged and for her cognitive and academic needs to be met. She asked "What's the point of going to school and who invented school anyway?!" Like her younger brother, she was self-taught and extremely advanced. There was no point for her to be in school, she reasoned, since she wasn't learning anything new. When she lamented, "If I remain in school, I'll never be able to be myself," it broke my heart.

Ritalin was offered as a solution to our kids' boredom, which was simply absurd. Once I learned about Ritalin and why schools were invented, I granted out kids' request to be homeschooled. School, as our then nine-year old daughter so aptly stated, is not about education, it's about control. Public school was modeled after the Industrial Revolution, the Prussian army, and B.F. Skinner's animal experiments. It has never been about fostering creativity and independent thinking and meeting the needs of **all** students.  Few people know that the founding fathers of education, John Dewey and B.F. Skinner, were members of the Socialist party.

This might explain why there are no federal mandates for gifted education. School districts decide what, if any, services they will provide. Since there is little agreement about who gifted students are or what they need, gifted students are often left to fend for themselves. Minority students are the least likely to be identified as gifted but the most likely to be identified as ADHD, or other special education labels (The National Association of Gifted Children, 2014). For these reasons, state and local homeschooling conferences began featuring workshops on homeschooling gifted students. As a speaker at these conferences, I noticed a huge increase in the number of minority families. Regardless of their race, parents were fed up.

**Does ADHD exist?**

It seems like everyone thinks they have ADHD and it is often used as an excuse for forgetfulness, inattention, disorganization, missing deadlines, impulsivity, and underachievement. It has become the ultimate blonde joke. But does it really exist? Before you stop reading, hear me out. The symptoms exist but, in my opinion, the disorder does not. The term *attention deficit disorder* or *ADD* was created by the American Psychiatric Association and was later changed to ADHD to include hyperactivity. Each drug that has come to market has created a big spike in ADHD diagnoses and an even bigger push for medication. ADHD studies were, and often still are, backed by the drug companies.

It really raised concerns by Dr. Peter Breggin, Harvard-trained psychiatrist and former full-time consultant at the National Institute of Mental Health (NIMH). He became a key witness in the subsequent class action lawsuits filed against the makers of Ritalin, Ciby-Geigy (now Novartis), the American Psychiatric Association, and the parent advocacy group CHADD. You can read more about Dr. Breggin and these cases at www.breggin.com.

As a parent of kids who were thought to have what was then called ADD, I received plenty of information. I knew something was up when I flipped over all the ADD brochures I received from teachers, psychologists, and CHADD. There were the drug companies' logos! I began to wonder if CHADD stood for *Ciba **Has** a **Direct Distributor***.

No one bothered to mention that Ritalin is a methamphetamine. It's a Type-II controlled substance nearly identical to cocaine. No one mentioned the side effects. Some of these are quite scary and can be permanent. In addition, no long-term studies have been done to determine the effects of stimulants on growing minds or bodies. Tens of thousands of gifted students were being mislabeled by their teachers and recommended for Ritalin.

Parents like me began catching on to this *left-brained conspiracy*. Since I was already blacklisted and our kids were no longer in the system, I decided to release my report. It was an evaluation of the gifted programming in all 50 schools in the Boulder Valley School District. There were huge disparities in the types of services offered, the identification procedures, and the use of funds. I sent it to the state department of gifted education and to Patti Johnson, who was the head of the Colorado State School Board. I mentioned the fact that many of these students were being mislabeled and recommended for Ritalin by their teachers.

In 1999, Colorado became the first state to acknowledge that too many students were being labeled ADHD and recommended for Ritalin. A resolution was passed and new assessment measures were established.

It is interesting to note that other members of the American psychiatric communities have made bold statements about

ADHD. Dr. Leon Eisenberg was reported as saying, "ADHD is a prime example of a fictitious disease" in an interview with the German magazine *Der Spiegel*.

Whether or not his comment was the result of a translation error or an over-zealous reporter remains the subject of debate. However, when Harvard psychologist Dr. Jerome Kagan was interviewed by the same magazine (English version), he clearly stated that "ADHD is an invention".

Once I discovered that there were many underlying issues causing ADHD symptoms in our kids and my young clients, I saw a pattern develop. I woke up in the middle of the night and mapped out a theory that later became known as *The Gifted/ADHD Connection.*

The biggest revelation was that the symptoms of ADHD and giftedness are **exactly the same**! I also saw that there was creativity or giftedness in one or both of the parents and determined that there were several underlying medical issues causing the symptoms, including allergies, asthma, food sensitivities, and hypoglycemia. What was the #1 trigger for all of these symptoms? Stress!

Here is a chart that I developed that illustrates the correlation:

| ADHD Symptoms (From the DSM-IV) | Gifted Characteristics (From The Gifted Development Center) |
|---|---|
| Has trouble paying attention and focusing | Active and vivid imagination |
| Daydreams; lost in own world | Hyper focuses on areas of interest – tunes out everything else |
| Fidgets, squirms in seat, cannot sit still | High energy level |
| Excessive talking | Advanced vocabulary |
| Impulsively blurts out answers in class | Quick mental abilities; often thinks 3 steps ahead |
| Often avoids, dislikes, or is reluctant to engage in tasks that require sustained mental ability | Advanced cognitive and/or creative abilities. Thrives on innovation and challenge, not repetitive tasks |

Notes:

*The DSM-IV = the Diagnostic and Statistical Manual of Mental Disorders, by the American Psychiatric Association. Known as "the APA bible", it is used to diagnose forms of mental illness and, apparently, learning differences.*

*The Gifted Development Center is located in Denver, Colorado, and is headed by Dr. Linda Silverman.*

From: *The Gifted/ADHD Connection.* Originally presented in March, 2000 at the NCGAT Conference in Winston-Salem, NC. Workshop title: *Harnessing Your Child's Potential Through Homeschooling. All rights reserved.*

I began to wonder: Is ADHD a hoax? Neurologist Dr. Fred Baughman really tells it like it is:

"Insofar as ADHD is concerned, it seems clear that in the '50s, as the first psychiatric drugs came to market, that psychiatry – in cahoots with the pharmaceutical industry – came upon the market strategy of, "Well, we'll call these things diseases." And the prototypical invented disease was called ADHD. So it's been a marketing strategy. This lie has been allowed to be published by the drug industry and by psychiatry, by our regulatory agencies, specifically the Food and Drug Administration. So that's where we are today."

So, in case you're wondering: "Why hasn't the public been told the truth?" the answer is money. As I stated in my blog post, *ADHD: What's Behind the Label?* , there is big money behind all this, as well as kickbacks, lobbyists, and loads of propaganda.

You can choose to agree with all this or not. Just know that you're not broken or defective! You're not dumb or lazy either. You just learn and experience the world differently. You may also be more sensitive and perceptive than most. And that's ok.

There is nothing wrong with being creative and having loads of ideas. Harnessing them is the trick! If your gifts and creativity were nurtured and valued in school or at home, more power to you! If not, know that you are not alone.

## Is giftedness really a gift?

While giftedness can be a blessing, it can also be a curse. It can also get us into trouble and can cause us to feel like we're out of sync from the rest of the world. Fitting in and conforming to the norm is a real challenge. We're not necessarily nerdy but we're also never part of the *in crowd*. I once saw a keychain that read "I'm not weird. I'm gifted." If you're uncomfortable with the word *gifted*, please accept my apologies. Some use the New Age terms *Indigos, Crystals,* or *Rainbows.* Labels, including *gifted,* aren't really necessary and can sometimes do more harm than good. I usually just go with creative and talented, since those terms don't push as many buttons.

It is very beneficial to be with others who are operating at a much higher level and who can motivate and encourage you. Once you're in the right environment, you can claim your giftedness and you can shine. I am so much more comfortable with musicians and on stage than at networking events or trying to fit into the corporate culture. How about you?

## *Take 5!*

Where do you feel "at home" or in your element? What are the types of activities and the types of people that make you feel the most comfortable?

### Testing, 1, 2....

You may be wondering at this point, "Should I be tested?" Keep in mind that IQ tests don't tell the whole story. They don't measure creativity, for example. They can also give false negatives. A false negative is a low score for someone who is obviously extremely bright. This happens to kids and adults for a variety of reasons. While students may need a certain IQ score to obtain services at their school, adults really don't need to bother, unless, of course, you feel the need to be a card-carrying member of Mensa, the genius society.

Personality tests like the Meyers-Briggs inventory can be useful but only to a point. The same applies to skills assessment tests. I have found both to be extremely limiting because you are only given a certain number of options. Since you're not allowed to add anything, you're forced to go with the choices that are available. The end result is therefore not entirely accurate. I have found the skills assessments and inventories to be the most limiting and frustrating, which is why I don't use any with my clients. The coaching process reveals what I need to know.

## How being a rebel is useful

In addition to birthing great inventions, products, and companies, rebels have also been very effective in social change. These are the people who have bucked the status quo and dared to ask questions like:

- ❖ Why can't developing countries have clean water?
- ❖ Why can't we prevent malaria easily and cheaply?
- ❖ Why can't we teach unemployed, homeless, or people in 3rd world countries how to start businesses?
- ❖ Why can't we help fund their endeavors with microloans or other sources of funding?
- ❖ Why can't we bring the arts to schools to increase creativity and self-esteem and decrease violence, stress, bullying, and depression?
- ❖ Why can't we make shoes and set the price a little higher, so we can donate a pair to someone in need with every purchase?

I can think of many more but you get the idea. You may have recognized some popular companies and easy solutions in these questions. What makes you want to scream a rebel yell could be a viable company or non-profit. You could even create a for-profit company which fuels your cause.

## The beat of your drum

Now, maybe you've started a business or you've begun to get your talent out there but nothing seems to be clicking. Either people don't get you or what you're about or you're just not sure if you're on the right path. I remember this phase well! What you need to do is dig deep. You need to figure out not only **what** you want to do but **why**.

I often have to ask my clients a series of questions in order to get down to the *why*. Your *why* is what will remind you of your true path. It will also keep you going on those days when you feel like banging your head against the wall. My *why* was discovered when I taught a career development class at a local women's homeless shelter. It was just four afternoons but it really opened my eyes to the real plight of the economy and the face of *the new homeless*. The new homeless were not the stereotypical drug addicts or people suffering from mental illness. These people previously had homes and good jobs. Some were making $80,000 a year. What happened?

Some got laid off or their husbands ran out on them and they could no longer pay the bills. Others had college degrees but just couldn't catch a break. Many people right now in our country are just one bill away from homelessness. It could be a large car repair or a medical bill. As I've learned from our own periods of layoffs and unemployment, it doesn't take much to throw everything in a tailspin. It's usually a series of unfortunate events. In some cases, it's bad decisions.

What I realized in those four afternoons was that, gifted or not, **everyone has potential**. In many cases, it's untapped potential. It wasn't until possibilities were presented that could combine with these ladies' gifts, that the light bulbs began to go off. I countered "I can't" with "Why not?" These ladies had no idea how much they could do with their amazing gifts.

I've taught at that shelter several times now. Every single class has had at least one artist, one dancer, one jewelry maker, and one musician. These women can only stay at the shelter for two months. I therefore don't think that it's just a coincidence that creative types just happen to be there when I come to teach. It's also not a coincidence that a friend who designed this class gave me this assignment when I was questioning my purpose and my existence and was struggling to hang on. My friend, and these ladies, had no idea.

It's also no coincidence that all of the struggles I've overcome from my childhood until now have prepared me to help others. They have also given me a new mission statement: I'd like to encourage, empower, and equip creative types to **RISE UP AND ROCK THE NEXT STAGE**!

So that's my *why*. And it was found right when I was about to give up.

**Finding your groove**

I started my business after I finished my first class at the homeless shelter. I had no idea whom I was going to market to or how I was going to do it. I just knew that I had the gift of encouragement and I could be a really good cheerleader and coach. I also had business and marketing skills, gleaned from my nearly 20 years of entrepreneurship, and I dusted off my MBA from 1985. I wish I could say that clients lined up right away but they didn't.

It was a constant process of trial and error and reinvention. I thought that I had a service that people would want but when things didn't magically take off, I began to wonder what the heck was going on. It was very frustrating and very discouraging. I almost gave up several times and felt like a total failure. I just couldn't find my groove and I didn't know why.

Know that you will have days when you wonder if you should just chuck it all and get a *real job*. Rebels don't do well working for others though, as I mentioned. Do you really want to be stuck in a dead-end job or in one that pays well but sucks the life out of you? Do you really want to help someone else build their dreams at the expense of yours? How long are you going to help a company make millions while you continue to be underpaid and undervalued?

I knew God had plans for me but to tell you the truth, it would've been a whole lot easier if He just plastered the instructions on a flashing neon sign! Maybe He did but I was too busy running in circles to see it. Have you ever done that? You're so busy being busy that you've forgotten what your mission was.

### *Take 5!*

1) So, what is your mission? Why do you want to break free and use your gifts and talents? What's your back story? Is happy, sad, or something in between? Is it bold, is it powerful, and does it command attention?

_______________________________________

_______________________________________

_______________________________________

_______________________________________

_______________________________________

_______________________________________

_______________________________________

_______________________________________

This is your drum beat. Once you identify it, you need to claim it. Write it down! If we were doing drum therapy or a drum circle together, I'd ask you to use the drum to express your feelings. I might even ask you what your mission sounds like and to tell me the story with your drum. This may provide you with the clarity you're seeking. It also is very freeing!

**No time like the present!**

2) Ok, so if you've written out your mission and think you'll save it for *someday*, I have to ask you a question: **What if you only had a year to live? What would you do?**

Think of all the things you've put off but really want to do. When I did this exercise, I realized what my problem was: I wasn't having any fun! Someone who plays drums and has a company called *Rock the Next Stage* should be a fun gal. Not someone who was tied to her computer and was so overwhelmed she could barely breathe.

When I saw my MRI results and researched my condition, I had a sudden sense of urgency. I sat at the computer stunned by the pictures of women who were thin and frail and could barely walk (It affects more women than men.). Once the cysts start invading your bones, you're in big trouble. I began considering exactly what I wanted to do before my conditioned worsened or my time was up and revised my bucket list.

The objective was to list 30 things. The first ten were easy and were all things I wanted to do with my business. Things got really interesting after that. Things popped out that were long buried. Others popped out that I had never really thought of before. When I read them, I thought "Well, that's cool!"

The problem with our society is that we focus on all the things we feel we **should** do. This is largely based on others' expectations or what we feel are societal norms. This is especially true for women. As one coach once told me, "Stop should-ing all over yourself!" It's true. How many people go to their deathbeds with regrets? Plenty!

No one ever puts "I wished I would have worked more" on their tombstone! In fact, working too much is one of the top 5 regrets that people have on their death bed, right up there with "I wish I'd let myself be happier" and "I wish I led a life true to my dreams" (Bronnie Ware, 2012).

Life's short! If you're not going to move forward with your hopes and dreams, then when do you plan on getting to them? There is no such thing as the perfect time, believe me! If you wait for the conditions to be completely perfect, you'll be waiting forever.

In my case, I knew I had to get better and stronger so I could hold my grandson. I also knew that there were loads of things I still wanted to do.

### *Take 5!*

1) What would be on your bucket list? Write out as many things that you can think of that you'd like to do. They can be personal, professional, or both. Grab a pad or a few sheets of paper and see if you can get up to 30. Writing, not typing, works better for this exercise.

2) If money were no object, what would you do? These can be things on your list or things that just popped into your head.

________________________________________________

________________________________________________

________________________________________________

________________________________________________

________________________________________________

________________________________________________

________________________________________________

________________________________________________

________________________________________________

_______________________________

_______________________________

86

_______________________________

_______________________________

3) Do you have a cause that you are passionate about?
You probably included it in your bucket list. Write it
below and explain why it's important to you.

_______________________________

_______________________________

_______________________________

_______________________________

_______________________________

_______________________________

_______________________________

_______________________________

_______________________________

_______________________________

_______________________________

_______________________________

**Allowing your song to unfold**

Part of allowing yourself to dream involves being open. That means paying attention to signs, gut feelings, people that suddenly appear in your space, and ideas that suddenly pop into your head. It's a lot like writing a song. You have to take some time to allow it to unfold.

This doesn't mean that every idea that you have will be from God or a Divine source. It doesn't even mean that it's good. Just let it sit for a while and see if it keeps coming back to you. Don't dismiss ideas or comments, just because you don't like them. Process them, let them sink in, pray, and meditate about them.

My brain was racing with so many thoughts that it was really hard to calm it down. It was also hard to hear what it was I needed to hear. Every day, I prayed, read my Bible, and wrote in my journal. But I felt like my words were just bouncing off the ceiling or getting stuck in the pages.

I hired coaches who kept telling me to "get clear". I thought: "You must be kidding. I've got 1,000 ideas in my head. Nothing is clear!" They asked me what God was saying. I told them that God wasn't saying anything. The real problem was I wasn't letting Him. I was doing all the talking. I had so much internal chatter that He probably couldn't get a word in edgewise!

And that's why sometimes God sends other people. I wasn't listening and I was being too stubborn. I wanted to figure out everything for myself; my symptoms, my business – everything. It took other people to gently point things out that I may have been missing.

Unfortunately, I wasn't sure that I believed them and things still weren't clear. Before the accident, I was pretty lucky. It was not uncommon for opportunities to find me. Now, it seemed like I couldn't get anything to click. Why?

I think it's because I doubted myself. I also doubted God. I knew He was there and but I wasn't sure why He wasn't making things happen. I got impatient and I kept grabbing at straws, trying to make things happen for myself.

The lesson I learned is that life is like brush strokes on a painting. You can't always see the effect until you step back. You're also not the true creator. Yes, you may have painted the painting but it was your Creator who gave you the talent and the idea. You also have to allow the paint to dry! Sometimes it takes longer than you expected.

The hardest thing for me was to learn to let go and to trust the process. I had a big vision. I could see it clearly. I kept pushing it away however. It was so big it was scary.

**Don't be afraid of your dreams! Embrace them! #findyourdivinerhythm**

I thought I had it all figured out. However, what I discovered was that, before I could more forward, there was much more inner work to be done.

**References and resources:**

*Right-brained Children in a Left-Brained World: Unlocking the Potential of Your ADD Child,* Jeffrey Freed and Laurie Parsons, ©1997, Simon & Shuster, pub. NY, NY

*Thom Hartmann's Complete Guide to ADHD,* ©2000, Thom Hartmann, Publisher's Group West

Dori Staehle

*Misdiagnosis and Dual-Diagnosis of Gifted Children and Adults*, Webb, Amend, et al, ©2005, Great Potential Press, Scotsdale, AZ

# Chapter 3
# Resetting Your Rhythm: Healing the Creative Soul

If you've lost your job, have a health issue, are starting a business, or are going through a period of transition, it's very common to feel stuck. I hear this complaint often in my travels and with new clients. In fact, after spending several months in Facebook and LinkedIn groups and seeing this complaint pop up over and over again, I decided I needed to write this book!

As someone who was stuck for several years, I can totally relate. I began telling my story and offering encouraging posts, tips, newsletters, and blogs. Through this process, I found healing. I also found answers.

**Repetitive beats**

Many creative types become stuck due to two major stumbling blocks: perfectionism and procrastination. For perfectionists, the pressure often doesn't come from an outside source; it comes from within. It's a little voice that tells you to re-write your newsletter or brochures, tweak (and re-tweak!) your website, video, or that book, painting, or song you've been working on.

Some of us procrastinate. We find other things that we feel we need to take care of like housework or errands or we allow ourselves to get sucked into the social media vortex. I'm not saying that you don't need to do the dishes or the laundry but when you keep pushing off your goals and your dreams, something is wrong.

When we are giving into procrastination or perfectionism, we are listening to that little voice that says that we are not enough. It may also be saying that our dreams are stupid and will never work out. This is the voice of fear. That little voice often grows into a giant, fire-breathing dragon.

No matter what you do, the dragon keeps reappearing and corners you so that you can't move forward. You feel stuck and are paralyzed by fear. You're afraid to release your project, business, or talent to the world. So, you put it off.

Something still feels missing though. You also know you're underachieving. All of this gets stuck in your head and even in the core of your being somewhere. You may not want to talk about it or even think about it, but it's there. It causes underlying stress, which can trigger many other conditions.

It's like you're constantly drumming to the same beat. You want to try something new and add something more interesting to the mix but you just can't seem to do anything else. Eventually, the beat slows down and starts to fade. Some people give up and leave those dreams on the shelf.

**Life on the dark side**

I realized that the reason people feel stuck is because they are holding onto something. It's tripping them up and they can't let go. When you feel stuck, you may also encounter anxiety or her evil twin depression. Both can set you so far back, it's tough to climb out.

Someone who is suffering from anxiety is generally worried about the future. They are plagued about all the "What if's". Thoughts generally go round and round. It's like having a constant spin cycle in your head.

People who are suffering from depression are often stuck in the past. Something happened that they can't release. Depression may be accompanied by sadness or anger, but it's actually a form of grief. The grief stems from something that's been lost. It could be a person, a job, or the person you once were. Both anxiety and depression can prevent you from moving forward and can steal your joy!

It's very common to have a case of the blues or even feel a little depressed after a major life change such as move, a job or career switch, or when the kids leave the nest. The problem is when the feeling stays for months (or years) or you begin having mood swings or crying jags. Is it hormones, depression, or something else? And why can't you shake it?

**Battling the demons**

There is a very high incidence of depression within the highly gifted and creative populations, which has been well documented. Many artists, musicians, singers, and comedians have taken their lives and joined what Courtney Love called *The Stupid Club*. The club contains her husband Kurt Cobain. Few know that Kurt, like many of those in this club, had a high IQ. Many also had unusual health issues and what was thought to be ADHD.

Highly gifted and creative people are also very sensitive to many external and internal stimuli. Clothing tags, sock seams, florescent lights, and certain smells and textures can really drive us nuts. As I discovered, hypoglycemia, allergies and asthma, and food allergies and sensitivities are highly prevalent as well. We're also very sensitive to feelings, both our own and those of others. All of this is much more prevalent in those who are predominantly right-brained.

We experience the world differently as well. What others can shake off easily may affect us deeply. Many are also extremely sensitive to things from the spiritual realm that most people don't see or sense. All of these factors can be most unsettling.

Those in the psychiatric community would have us believe that depression is a form of mental illness. I feel that is a spiritual illness, combined with medical issues which have been triggered by stress. All I know is that there is a battle going on and the voices that a person may hear are not in their head. They are real.

It's definitely not God talking though. It's entities from a much darker place. God would never tell you that you are worthless, your dreams are stupid, or that you should end it all. Whether you call it Satan, the devil, Beelzebub, or demons is irrelevant. There really is a dark side. I've been there and I've sensed it around others.

Several of my young band members attempted suicide and several tutoring students developed depression or anorexia. I stood in the gap and prayed for protection for them. Prayer, resolve, and faith are powerful antidotes to fear. All of these kids survived and are now leading happy lives.

## *Take 5!*

If you are in this place now, don't you dare give up! The world needs you and what you have to offer! You are valued and were created for a purpose. Put this book down right now and take some deep breaths. Ask God, Jesus, Spirit, and the angels in heaven to protect you.

Release all of that regret, disappointment, and shame that you've been holding onto. It's time. It's time to move on. You don't need this burden anymore. It's not serving you in any way. Give it to God. Send those negative feelings packing!

If you can't do this alone, reach out and ask for help! Call a friend, a family member, a pastor, or someone from your church. Don't wait. Do it now.

**The beat goes on**

If you're a creative type, you have probably have gone through life thinking that no one gets you and that you don't fit in. It can be very lonely and disheartening. You may have also been keeping everything in because you feel that you don't want to burden anyone with your problems or you don't want to scare them.

You might also be worried that if anyone knew that you were struggling, people would know the real truth. Maybe you've been faking it for a long time and you've worked really hard at maintaining that perfect image. You may think that if you told anyone, they would know that you don't have it all together. Maybe you're extremely disappointed in yourself, not to mention embarrassed. You're afraid to say anything to anyone because you know you'll start crying and well, that would be even more embarrassing!

I knew that I had to get a handle on this and get to the bottom of it if I was going to rise above it. Just like with *The Gifted/ADHD Connection*, I knew that there were some missing pieces to the puzzle. I'm about to get a little deep here, so buckle up. The good news is that the beat goes on!

**Your personal rhythm**

One reason that people aren't moving forward is because there is an imbalance in their personal rhythm. When something seems a little off, people are known to say they feel *out of sync*.

People who are struggling or fighting with one another are *not in harmony* with each other. Our lives are filled with music and rhythm. It's all part of the dance.

Every cell in your body is pulsating with energy and has its own rhythm. Your heartbeat has a certain rhythm. The blood flowing in and out of your veins is doing so in rhythm. There are  electrical impulses traveling through your body as well. This static electricity can cause you to get a shock when you touch someone or rub your feet on the carpet.

Your brain is not only firing electrical impulses rapidly but it's also recording your experiences. What you may not realize is that the cells of your body are recording and absorbing those experiences as well. Every experience you've ever had, every thought you've processed, every word that you've been told or said has carried a certain weight, a certain rhythm, and a certain energy.

Some things may have passed through quickly and virtually unnoticed but others have managed to stick. It's not only the event, word, or picture that your brain registers; it's your **perception** of that event, word, or picture. This negative energy and stress can lodge itself in your body and create blockages. It therefore stands to reason that these blockages can cause inflammation, allergies, asthma, and eventually cysts, or even tumors. As I've proven, you don't have to be stuck with all this!

Being in a family, work, or educational environment that doesn't value you can cause years of stress. This creates havoc to your central nervous system, causing the fight or flight response, making you perpetually feel on high alert.

Stress is the trigger for many conditions, including ADHD-like symptoms, as I previously discussed. It's a shame that this can start as soon as gifted, talented, and creative kids enter school but it's true. In fairness, it's impossible for most schools to meet the needs of all children, especially those who are exceptionally gifted, talented, and creative. In some cases, the stress comes from home or outside events.

"Good stress", like the excitement of a new challenge, can be beneficial and can fuel creativity. However, "bad stress", especially on a consistent basis, can kill creativity. Here is an excerpt from a blog post I wrote called *The Death of Creativity*, which explains some of the history of education but can also be applied to what happens in the work world and, some may say, in our government:

*Public schools were established during the Industrial Revolution to warehouse the children of the factory workers and to train them for the same assembly lines. Public schools also trained students to be the ultimate consumers and to be forever dependent on the system. The government is still deciding how and what children should learn. What's the point of creating students who can take tests but who can't think for themselves? Maybe that **is** the point. Public school was, and still is, an experiment in social engineering.*

These realizations fueled my decision to leave teaching and my company, *Next Stage Educational Services*. I just couldn't deal with the schools anymore or the students who were stressed out, burned out, and unable to think outside the box. I had seen a dramatic decline in creative thinking. Consequently, brainstorming abilities were nearly non-existent. Students are limited by the type of formulaic learning that has become the by-product of standardized education. Forget creativity! It's all about teaching to the test.

I wondered, "If all this negativity and stress was being lodged into the cells of their bodies, what would happen to these kids as they got older?" Our educational system was not encouraging creative careers or entrepreneurism. I thought, "Wait until they find out that, after they graduate from college, they get to work in cubicles and become more stressed out and frustrated. They get to work in yet another environment that generally doesn't value individuality or creativity and wants you to do the job of five different people for the price of one!"

No wonder our nation has such a high rate of heart attacks, stroke, cancer, depression, and suicide! What if there were natural ways to avoid all of this? Actually, there are. Big Pharma, Big Government, and Big Healthcare just don't want you to know about them.

**Alternative medicine**

If you are feeling stressed out and can't focus, this could be the result of one or more of the above issues. Fortunately, there are many natural alternatives that can alleviate the effects of stress.

Alternative medicine practices such as Healing Touch, Reiki, Qigong, acupuncture, and chiropractic can detect underlying issues, as well as pain and blockages of energy, and can restore balance.

I have recently heard of *sound therapy* which uses either a tuning fork or a *singing bowl*. Both date back to ancient times and emit certain frequencies conducive to healing. There are also a growing number of companies offering essential oils, which date back to biblical times.

When I first began training in Healing Touch, I could easily detect the areas of pain without even touching the person's body. Healing Touch is a form of energy medicine, which, like therapeutic drumming, is also used in hospitals and is based on extensive research and established protocols. When the person is on the massage table, I close my eyes and I see certain colors. For me, red and orange indicate pain.

It's possible that I am sensing vibrations from the person's body, which causes certain colors for me. Some musicians actually see colors in musical notes. Each note vibrates at a certain frequency, which produces a certain color. The ability to sense colors is called *synesthesia* and is apparently a rare neurological phenomenon (*Mauer and Mondlach, 2002 and Gray, 2005*). When you think about it, we use colors to describe how we're feeling. If you're sad, you feel blue. Maybe it has to do with your vibration.

If you're freaking out right about now and thinking that this is too New Agey, just remember that the well-accepted practices of yoga and chiropractic were once thought to be way out there. As for energy medicine, keep in mind that Jesus and his disciples were healers and practiced the laying on of hands. Prayer is also a form of energy healing.

**Universal rhythm**

Everything that has cells vibrates and has a frequency and a pitch. You just can't hear it with the human ear. The planets rotate on their axes and travel through their orbits at different speeds. Scientists have actually detected certain frequencies from the planets. I would imagine there would be frequencies in the stars as well, especially the sun due to solar activity. If anyone ever charted out all the notes, that would be one cool symphony!

Therefore, the entire world is music - designed by the Divine Composer. We are all connected by music. It's the universal language and the universal healer.  If you could change people's rhythms, you could change their lives and perhaps the lives of those around them.

## Removing blockages

When you can't seem to get past something, it's possible that it has caused a blockage. It could also be a trigger from a past experience. If something is making you feel disappointed, sad, or betrayed, it could be a past event that produced that feeling. You may not even remember it because it was so long ago.

There are studies which have investigated the effect of stress on various cultures and races. This is called *epigenetics* and is quite fascinating. It was the topic of my friend and colleague Shella Zelenz's dissertation, which will soon be produced in the form of a documentary called *RootEd*. I was one of the interviewees for this film.

What you need to ask yourself when negative thoughts or behaviors creep in is the following:

1) Where is this coming from?
2) When have I felt this way before?
3) What happened to make me feel this way or believe this?

If you think this is *psycho-babble* or just too weird, have you ever been given some bad news and felt it right in the pit of your stomach? Well, technically it's in your solar plexus, but you get the idea. It feels like someone just socked you in the gut, doesn't it?

So, if you've been thrown a curveball recently and you're wallowing in negativity and uncertainty, that's because your personal rhythm has been thrown off! That's why you don't feel connected anymore. Maybe you've felt this way for a long time.

It took me quite some time to realize that all of this was wrapped up in my feeling stuck as well. I did not realize that I had been carrying so much pain, disappointment, and anger about the accident and its aftermath, nor did I realize that I had developed the symptoms of post-traumatic stress disorder, or PTSD. It wasn't the accident itself but the constant harassment and berating by the insurance company and the doctors, as well as the feeling of betrayal from my employer. I would almost hyperventilate when an email or phone call would come in from any of the individuals I had to deal with. Welcome to the world of worker's compensation, where the accident victim has no rights and is assumed to be faking.

As a result, doctor visits would make me fearful, stressed out, and raise my blood pressure. It was apparent that they did not believe that I was telling the truth about my pain levels or my symptoms, nor did they look at my complete file or medical history.  Nurses and an insurance representative yelled at me. I was constantly questioned and ridiculed.  It was almost like being abused all over again. My personality began changing into someone I no longer recognized.

Past hurts can haunt you for some time without you even realizing it. They sneak up on you when you least expect it and can become the proverbial straw that broke the camel's back.

**Time to recalibrate!**

How do you snap out of it? **You need to reset your rhythm!** It's like when you veer off course or miss an exit while driving and your GPS has to recalibrate. One way to do this is through therapeutic drumming, of course. **You also need to retrain your brain. Replace all that negative garbage with positive thoughts!**

What is also extremely effective is to hang around with positive, successful people. Believe it or not, you will begin to match their rhythm, their energy, and their frequency. This is called *entrainment*. The more positive, upbeat, and confident you are, the more you will attract people who not only get you, they want to work with you!

Entrainment can also occur affect the cycles of women in a tribe or even in a college dormitory. Entrainment happens when drumming in a group as well. Eventually, the rhythms will naturally begin to match.  When people are worried that they don't know how to drum or they feel they don't have any rhythm, I tell them not to worry. Entrainment will pull them to the beat.

There is also something known as binaural beat entrainment which involves listening to two different frequencies at once. Eventually, these two frequencies blend into a third frequency (Kasprzak, 2011). Binaural beat entrainment is said to help with psychomotor performance and mood (Lane, Owens, and

Marsh, 1998).

The reason that many creative, ADHD types feel so out of synch is because they are! If you're in an educational or professional environment that doesn't match your personal energy, style, your abilities, or your rhythm, you'll always feel like you don't belong. Once you find your tribe or your flock, you will blossom. God loves you just the way you are. You don't need to keep beating yourself up for being different. Embrace your uniqueness and keep marching to the beat of your own drum!

Once I accepted the fact that I didn't have to be what everyone wanted me to be and that I could do what I love and what brought me joy, peace came over me. It can happen to you as well.

**Calming things down**

I like working with kids with ADHD traits or Asperger's because they, like me, have a really high energy level. I joke that we're not hyper; we just spin at a different frequency! And that is actually true.

Ever notice how many ADHD types are thin? That's because we have super-high metabolisms! Yes, my friends who are dieting hate me, especially when they see how often I have to eat. If you're feeling sluggish, stuck, cranky, have headaches or stomach aches, or are suffering from "brain fog", it could be what you're eating.

In fact, many gifted/ADHD types have hypoglycemia (low blood sugar) but don't know it. The remedy is to eat certain things at certain times. I've been eating this way for decades and it's a great way to reduce my hypoglycemia symptoms, increase my energy and focus, and stabilize my blood sugar levels so that I don't have energy or mood swings.

**Here are some dietary tips that may help*:**

- ❖ Eat 3 healthy meals a day + 3 high protein snacks.
- ❖ Avoid caffeine and sugar after 6 pm.
- ❖ Reduce or eliminate processed sugar. Stick with natural alternatives, such as fruit and agave nectar. Limit fruit juice! Natural fruit juice mixed with club soda is ok.
- ❖ Eliminate preservatives. Processed food contains tons of sodium and preservatives which are bad for your body – and your brain!

- ❖ Take high potency multivitamins. You may also need some supplements in case you have mineral deficiencies (Low iron, magnesium, and zinc is very common with ADHD types) or you need help with focusing.
- ❖ If you're super stressed out, chances are your adrenals are shot and you'll need extra vitamin B or B-complex.
- ❖ Stop eating junk and ditch the soda and super sugary and highly caloric coffee drinks!

*Disclaimer: This does not constitute medical advice. Consult with a professional before making any changes. Sudden discontinuation of stimulants can cause withdrawal symptoms.

## *Take 5!*

**Try keeping a food journal for a week**. Write down everything you eat and drink but pay close attention to how you felt afterwards. Also note that what you crave tends to indicate what you shouldn't have, especially if you have hypoglycemia or food allergies and sensitivities!

- ❖ Did you feel hyperactive?

❖ Did your energy spike but then crash 30 minutes after you ate (an indication of reactive hypoglycemia)?

❖ Did you frequently crave sugar and carbs (possible indication of hypoglycemia or diabetes)?

❖ Did your stomach hurt or did you feel bloated (possible food or gluten allergies)?

**Learning to relax**

In our fast-paced, super-charged world, it seems like we never relax. We're always on the go and we're always connected to some type of digital device. In fact, I almost got rear-ended today, because the driver behind me was looking down at her cell phone and didn't see that I had stopped!

If you've been under stress or if you're just normally hyperactive, your central nervous system is on high alert. It needs to be calmed down so you can give your body and brain a rest and so you can heal any cells in your body that need to be healed. Here are some suggestions to help you get started:

❖ Don't grab your cell phone the first thing in the morning! Email and social media can wait! Instead, take some time to sit still, calm your thoughts, meditate, or pray.

- ❖ Write in a journal. Also try to listen for any ideas or messages. Go to a quiet place, if you have to.
- ❖ Drink plenty of water. Start in the morning and continue during the day. Add lemon or lime for added flavor and benefits.
- ❖ Do your most creative things first.
- ❖ Get physical! Walk, jog, swim, shoot hoops, bike, do yoga, or whatever works for you.
- ❖ Go out in nature and enjoy God's creation! Take your camera or sketchpad, if you like!
- ❖ Take frequent breaks to give your eyes and your brain a rest. Stretch, look out the window, or even daydream a bit.
- ❖ Listen to music, depending on your mood and what needs to get done.
- ❖ Take time to drum!

**How drumming works**

In addition to blowing off steam, drumming can have the following benefits:

- ❖ Reduction in hyperactivity
- ❖ Increased focusing capability
- ❖ Reduced anxiety and stress
- ❖ Increased clarity and creativity
- ❖ Improved memory
- ❖ Boosts the immune system

- ❖ Reduces employee turnover and burnout
- ❖ Improved school/work performance
- ❖ Improved self-esteem
- ❖ Improved student behavior
- ❖ Burns calories
- ❖ Produces spontaneous laughter and fun!

Drumming helps to sync up the left and right hemispheres of the brain and makes the individual feel more connected. The vibration of drums and percussion instruments in group drumming sessions has been proven to also help with healing. Drum therapy is used in hospitals, nursing homes, community centers, and schools, using established protocols based on scientific research.

Drumming can be done using flat drums, buffalo drums, bongos, congas, or African drums such as Djembes (pronounced *Jem-bay*). Percussion instruments such as shakers, maracas, cowbell, or claves (pronounced *klah-vays*) can be used as well. For healing and therapy, I prefer using a Djembe. You can drum by yourself but it's even more fun and effective to drum with others.

A trained therapeutic drumming facilitator or drum therapist will incorporate certain rhythms and techniques depending on what needs to be achieved. Some, like me, may also include counseling or specific healing techniques. The drumming community includes people of all faiths and spiritual backgrounds. Some tap into that more than others. Some don't use it at all. Others use the title *drum healer*, if they are using their gifts of intuition and healing. I am learning to embrace this title for myself.

The repetitive nature and patterns of the beats can reset your rhythm, clear blockages, improve circulation, and coordination, and even help you burn some calories! Healing benefits have even been seen in people who just observed but didn't drum. Actually whacking on a drum is much more fun, however. For those of us with a brain full of too many thoughts and ideas, drumming can actually produce clarity and calmness.

Drum therapy is an interactive form of music therapy, which also combines occupational therapy and energy medicine. It's not a music lesson and the goal is not to go on tour with Santana or Bruno Mars (although that would be cool!). Here's a description of a typical session:

## What a drumming session is like

For my private sessions, I use Djembes. The student/client has one and I have one. This could be in-person or virtual, although in-person works better. If it's in person, they can use one of my drums or they can bring their own.

If a Djembe is being used, it needs to be placed between the knees and tipped forward slightly. You need to tilt it away from your body for better hand positioning and so that the sound can come out of the bottom. If the drum is flat on the floor, you won't get the vibration or the tone that you need. This also limits the sound waves and vibrations, so you won't get the full healing benefits.

You'll notice that the center of the drum has a nice, rich tone, which is your *bass*. The edges have another tone, which is the *slap*. You can alternate between the two. You can also do an open tone or mute the sound with one hand. As for me, I'm all about that bass. It's very addictive. I add in lots of bass when I play.

If you're using bongos, those can be on your lap or attached to a metal bongo stand, like what the professionals use.  Just like the Djembe, bongos have holes on the bottom which shouldn't be blocked. If they're on your lap, you can position your legs so that some sound is coming out of the bottom of the bongos.

If you're using flat drums, you'll need to hold it up and put it on one leg like a steering wheel. The flat side should be facing out and the open side should be facing your body. You can also dance or walk around with a flat drum. You can tap out beats with your hands or a mallet, if you have one. There are all sorts of cool rhythms you can do with your fingers as well.

If the client or student has sound sensitivities, has dexterity issues, or is just fearful of drumming for some reason, I may use shakers, claves, or a small, flat drum known as a *sound shape*, which comes with a small stick. I use these mainly with kids but sometimes adults like them as well. I usually tap out a beat and have them follow, in a call and response type of pattern. I'll start adding beats to make it more challenging or ask them to add something. It sounds pretty cool and can help them with coordination and listening skills. We may also jam a bit at the end, just for fun.

If you combine all of this in a group, get ready to rock! It can be loud but it's a blast! I'll lead the group and teach everyone simple beats and then they'll add extra parts when they feel comfortable. Some people may get to bust out a solo, if they're up for it. There might be singing or affirmations, depending on the purpose of the group. I generally don't sing but I might make sounds with my voice to signify what their part should sound like. Percussionists are good with sound effects! I haven't used singing bowls yet but some drum healers add them to their sessions.

Drum healing is different and can be conducted like a Reiki, or energy healing session. In this case, I may drum around or near the person while the person is sitting down. The recipient can also be lying down. The techniques used depend on what the drum healer senses is needed. Drum healing can be included with a Reiki session as well.

As for the people who think that drummers should be male, consider this fact: The first drummers were women (1). Back in ancient times, women led worship with flat drums that were like large tambourines and may have been translated as such. In fact, music and musical instruments are mentioned throughout the Bible. Drumming is not from the devil, it's not voodoo, you're not conjuring up evil spirits, and it's not a "hippie thing".

Yes, you can be a Christian and a drummer, drum therapist, drum circle facilitator, or even a drum healer. Tie-dyed shirts, bandanas, and hippie beads are not required. I've heard it all, so I thought I'd get that out of the way.

## The effects of drumming

I had no idea how deeply moved I would be by drumming after the accident. It became a great way to vent my feelings of anger and frustration. I have to confess that some days I drummed until tears streamed down my face. My hands might have turned red but I kept going. As my beats slowed down, so did my breathing. I always felt much better afterwards. It is no wonder that drumming works so well with at-risk kids and adults!

Drumming affects people differently and can be used for different reasons. In addition to fun drumming events and individual drum therapy, drumming is also used to improve communication in families and within organizations. This involves more talking to get people to drum out their feelings.

Different beats can represent different things. Each individual tends to represent what they're feeling in a different way, so this can be interesting. Some companies use drumming for team-building events. Different cultures also drum differently. Latin beats are different from African beats, for example. Understanding and embracing differences can be done through music.

Drumming can also be very freeing! If I see people being really timid and reserved with the drums, I give them permission to whack on the drums as fast and hard as they like. Once they start, they really get into it! Drumming has been used after traumatic events like school shootings and has been used for conflict resolution and anger management with student populations, as well as for post-traumatic stress disorder for veterans (2).

When I'm facilitating a session that is supposed to be therapeutic, I tell people that it's a safe space. What happens during a session stays in the session. You may need to cry – or get in touch with your confidence, power, and inner drum chick or drum dude!!

Take a walk on the wide side! You've been holding back long enough!

 **Have some fun! Whack on a drum!**
**#findyourdivinerhythm**

## Drum Therapy Articles and Research

You can find an extensive list of links about drumming and research on my website:
www.rockthenextstage.com/drumming

**References:**


1) *When the Drummers were Women: A Spiritual History of Rhythm*, by Layne Redmond, ©1997, Three Rivers Press.

2) *Rhythm Healing: PTSD, Trauma, and Beyond*, by D.W. (Bill) Moore, RE, ©2013 (self-published)

# Chapter 4
# Power Surge: Rock What You've Got!

Ok, now it's time to pick up the tempo! I hope you're ready! It's time to get in touch with your gifts and talents. They're calling. And they want you back. Is there something you used to love to do that you're not doing anymore? Do you miss it? Here's a test:

Whenever the arts have been removed from my life, it felt like part of me died. Sure, you can try to suck it up and get used to it but you never really do. The true test of this is to pick up something you haven't done in a while. Get that guitar out of your closet or find your old sketchpads and paints. Now, start playing or painting and see how you feel. It not only warms your heart but it just might make you cry. It will if you miss it terribly.

It also can help you get unstuck. It's like the missing piece. That's how I knew I needed to get back into the church band. I had resigned myself to the fact that my injuries might prevent me from playing for a long time. At that point, there was the possibility that they were permanent.

Then, as my husband and I were driving one day, a tune came on the radio that the band used to play. Once the guitar solo kicked in, I thought of our lead guitarist. And I totally lost it. Tears kept streaming down as I realized that I missed the band members and I missed playing. It's a good thing Mark was driving because I was a mess! I had been away from the band for a year and a half. Even though I wasn't entirely healed at that point, I knew I had to go back.

When you're going about your daily activities, it's easy to push your hopes, dreams, talent, and creativity aside. They may be quiet but they're still there. In fact, you may have dismissed them but others might detect them. Have your friends ever commented on something you do well? Do they push you and suggest that you do that activity again or convert it into a business or career?

## *Take 5!*

What do you do best or what comes easy to you? What do you do naturally for friends that could possibly become a business or career?

**Crank it up to 11!**

If you've been hiding your gifts or downplaying them, now's the time to start releasing them. It's time to crank it up to 11 and rock what you've got! Everyone has something special and unique to offer that makes them stand out. This can become part of your signature style and your "calling card", so to speak. It's all about figuring out what you stand for – and what people remember. This is all part of branding.

Many of the bands and solo artists I worked with hated it when I used this term. They would say things like "I'm not a business or a product!"

Actually, they are. All entrepreneurs and creative types are a business. You are your brand. You are also in the business of sales. You are not just selling your products or services. You are selling yourself to prospective clients or fans! It's the same with job seekers. Once you enter the interview room, you have to sell the prospective employer on YOU! And guess what? You only have about 30 seconds.

You have to stand out quickly if you want to be remembered and if you want people to stay interested enough to find out more. For websites, you actually only have about ten seconds to grab visitors' attentions, otherwise they will bounce.

Branding is more than just a website or your logo; it's about the person behind the brand. An example of someone who has branded herself really well and knows all about marketing and positioning is Taylor Swift. I'd also give her extra bonus points for the amazing ways she's used social media to reach out to her fans.

## It's a matter of perception

What people **perceive** about you is actually your personal brand. In my case, people commented on the following: My rocker chick hair and clothes, my jewelry, and my energy. Many also remember that I drum. Yes, the first three things are pretty shallow but at least they remembered something!

What words come to mind when you see the Starbucks® logo?

An expensive cup of coffee! It's also stronger than many other brands. It's a totally different image than say, Dunkin' Donuts® coffee, which focuses more on value, and well, donuts. The ambience of their stores is much different, as is the clientele.

It's therefore very important to be "on brand". In order to do that, you need to figure out what your brand is! For example, when I only talked about ADHD symptoms and drumming as a natural alternative, people thought I only worked with kids. Another mistake I made was switching up my elevator pitch and my title. One week, I'd be a personal branding specialist. The next week, I was *Dori the Drum Chick* and the following week I was a business and success coach.

I needed to figure out what I was offering and explain it in a very clear and concise way. That meant deciding what kind of coach I was. I also needed to show them the real Dori.  I got tired of men telling me to stop talking about the drumming: "You've got an MBA! You're supposed to be a business coach. You've got to lose the drum chick schtick!"

The gauntlet had been thrown. I decided to accept this as a personal challenge.  I started by doing something to my hair that I always wanted to do. I added hot pink highlights. It was just an experiment. I bought a jar of *Manic Panic®* dye from the local beauty supply store and painted hot pink streaks onto my hair with a small paintbrush. What I discovered was that you can purchase a whole lot of attitude for just $11!

I brought a drum and an "I really don't care what you think" attitude to a networking meeting. My new elevator pitch was pretty funny. What was even funnier was that women actually started coming over to ask me about the drumming! If my goal was to help people heal and move forward with drumming, then I decided I'd say yes to as many drumming opportunities as I could.

And boy, did they roll in! In the span of two months, I did more drumming events than I had done all year. Yes, some were free but some actually paid pretty well. I drummed for kids and adults, both outside and inside. I even drummed on a beautiful lake on a pontoon boat. It was a two-hour cruise, complete with champagne and appetizers. "I can get used to this!" I thought.

The real Dori was finally starting to re-appear. It was about time! Since I now had more money, I went to a salon to get real hot pink highlights. While I may not be booking huge concerts anymore, that doesn't mean that I need to totally bury that side of my personality.

All I know is that when I drum and help people, or even talk about drumming and helping people, I'm told that I light up. I found what I had lost after my accident. I found my joy. And I realized that I can't drop the drumming. It's too much a part of me - and my brand.

**Singing the right tune**

One of the things I do for bands and creative entrepreneurs is to see if their image matches their message, industry, or genre. For example, I've been fooled by bands whose look screams punk or metal but their music is pop. Or, worse yet, they have a really great look but they haven't taken the time to learn how to sing or play.

They seem to think that if they get the right clothes and use a pitch modulator when they record, no one will notice that they really can't sing. Or how about the Christian band who turned and prayed on stage right before they started their first song, only to later slip and drop the "F-bomb"- during a song?! I called the lead singer out and told him that he violated one of my (and the venue's) rules and wouldn't be paid. He proceeded to pitch a fit and told me that everyone uses that word. Wrong answer! He also proceeded to continue to argue with me via email. This was not a good first impression, needless to say.

If you're going to walk the walk, you've got to talk the talk! I didn't like his attitude, so I had to tell the band that I couldn't continue to book them. They were the only Christian band on the roster that night. The metal and hardcore bands were more respectful. So much for stereotypes. Since these were all-ages shows, I felt the bands needed to be mindful of the fact that sometimes there were young kids in the audience. This is a good idea for adult bands as well, especially at outdoor events where your voice really travels.

## *Take 5!*

What image are you trying to convey? What word or words do you represent? If you don't know, take a poll. Ask people via email or online what words come to mind. Don't ask just anyone. Ask people who know you and who can give a fair assessment.

Are these words reflected in your photos, website, business cards, and other materials? What about your book or CD cover? How about the inserts and images? Is the message clear and consistent? If not, you have a branding problem. You may need to update your look, try different colors or accessories, change your poses or facial expression, and use better graphics or images for your print and online materials.

I've helped many coaching clients create a consistent and effective brand, including their wardrobe, makeup, and jewelry choices. Branding goes way beyond your logo, color choices on your website, or well-written copy. It's also about how you feel about yourself. Marketing and branding tips won't add up to much if you lack confidence and aren't ready to step into your greatness.

**What's in a name?**

It's important to choose a business or band name that matches your brand. You need to make sure it's not already being used. The same applies to your logo.

I started with a Google search. My first choice was *Rock Your Biz*. I checked a domain registry and the name was available. I made the mistake of waiting three days before I signed back on to purchase the domain name. In three days, someone came out of the woodwork and snatched it up! I have to admit, I was pretty ticked off.

I clicked the link to see who took the name. A picture popped up of a middle-aged bald guy. "I bet he's never rocked a day in his life!" I yelled at my computer screen. I later discovered that many people have used the word rock in their company name or program. I joke that I am the only one who actually does rock out on a regular basis.

The good news is that once my business model began to take shape, *Rock the Next Stage* is actually a better fit.

**Tip**: Don't wait too long to grab a domain name. Do your research to make sure no one has it and then register and pay for it. Like they say, "Ya snooze, ya lose!" It's a good idea to also grab the .biz, .net, and the .org, if you can swing it. Domain names usually run $6-$11 each (per year). Securing them prevents someone else from trying to use your name. Authors and speakers often reserve their own name, in addition to their company name, so that no one can claim to be them.

**Bands**: You also should do a search to see if anyone has your intended band name. If a name pops up, don't dismiss it thinking that it's no big deal because they're in another state. If the band is signed, you absolutely cannot use their name! This is copyright infringement and you could be sued. The same applies for logos and photos.

Also, it's a good idea to check your acronym. Make sure it's not something that someone else has like UPS®. Make doubly sure it doesn't spell out something questionable. A local Christian band has a great name but the initials spell out *WTF*. The band was formed before this acronym became popular. Either way, it's not the best scenario for a Christian band and cannot appear in their logo (For those who somehow don't know what this widely popular and over-used acronym is, it's "What the f---?"). It might be funny for another band but it just doesn't work in this case.

Finally, don't pick a name that's:
1) Too long!
2) Tough to spell or a really weird spelling.
3) Is really someone else's company name but you just added a hyphen.

4) Doesn't tie into what you do. It can be different but you'll need to add a good tagline or slogan.

**Tip:** Test the name out on a few people before locking it down! If it doesn't make sense and no one gets it, you have a problem. Here are a few comments I got from *Rock the Next Stage*:

1) "You're booking bands again?"
2) "Oh! You're coaching speakers?" (Not then but I am now!)
3) "The next stage? You mean like the afterlife?" (You can't make this stuff up, people!)

That's why I needed a good tagline.

## *Take 5!*

*Brainstorming time! Write down 10 possible names. And...go!*

If you start checking out your competition, either in –person or online, don't try to be an exact copy! Comparison may be the greatest form of flattery but it can also be the thief of joy if you convince yourself that you don't measure up.

**Be yourself! Don't try to copy someone else's look, style, or sound.  #findyourdivinerhythm**

That's how you stand out from the crowd. There will always be tons of people who do what you do. Don't get discouraged by this! Instead, find what makes you unique and capitalize on that. It also helps to keep your website easy to read and navigate. Resist the urge to clutter it up with too much text. You don't want to overwhelm or confuse people. Keep it simple.

**What happens when you say "Yes" to your gifts and your dreams**

Switching gears and second-guessing yourself are great ways to stall your dreams. They are definitely forms of self-sabotage. Nothing will slow you down faster. You stopped trusting your intuition and you're letting fear control you.

Everyone has intuition. It's that feeling in the pit of your stomach or the hairs that stand up on the back of your neck when you sense danger. It can also tell you who you should and shouldn't trust. It can also lead us to some really good opportunities as well.

Problems arise, however, when you don't trust yourself.  It can also mean you don't trust God. God never gives you a dream or a vision that He doesn't think you can handle. He has chosen you for a reason and has given you (or will give you) everything you need to succeed. Imagine if someone gave you a gift but, instead of opening it, you decided to tuck it away in the closet? How do you think the giver of the gift would feel?

When you have a dream or an idea but don't act upon it, guess what happens? Sooner or later, that assignment will be given to someone else who is going to take it and run with it. I can't tell you how many ideas I had for inventions but didn't follow through. Eventually, someone else did. I still cringe when I see these items on the shelves at major retailers.

The same applies to guest speakers and musicians. Have you ever sat in the audience and thought "I can do a better job that that!"? Well, guess what? You're in the audience and that person is on the stage. They're getting paid and you're not. If you think you can do better, prove it! It's time to stop complaining and take action.

## *Take 5!*

Write down a list of things you intended to do but didn't or started but didn't finish. Now, pick three that you are still passionate about and you could start right now. Write them down here:

_____________________________________________

_____________________________________________

_____________________________________________

_____________________________________________

### The cost of being stuck

If you've taken any business classes, you may have heard of the principal of *lost opportunity cost*. You don't need to have an MBA to figure this out, however. Just take into account when you didn't take action on and what it has cost you. It could be a monetary value or an intangible item, like peace of mind, or both.

For example, say you're a solo artist, you're a speaker, or you're in a band.  Either way, you know you can earn money in various ways: 1) Booking gigs, 2) Selling stuff at your gigs, and 3) Selling your stuff online.

However, many people don't map out a game plan, don't put together a contract, and take any gig that comes along, even if it doesn't pay. Those who take free gigs generally do so because they didn't bother to ask about payment. Many of us have gotten sucked into working for free because the organizer claimed it would be *good exposure*. Imagine hiring an electrician but telling him that you can't afford to pay him but hey, having his van in your driveway is good exposure for his business. Yeah, right! He won't even bother to show up. Why, then, do people think that the rest of us will work for free?!

Knowing how the game is played or hiring someone to help you can really boost your income. If you don't sell yourself enough and or hire anyone to sell you, it's really hard to cover your expenses. For each gig, you need to spend money on gas, extra strings or drumsticks (or copies of your handouts, if you're a speaker), food and beverages, and maybe even hotel rooms. How much money do you technically lose by taking free or low-paying gigs? You don't want to know. Now, if the free gigs got you a paying gig after the fact, that's another story. However, you still lost money.

But wait! There's more! If you took a bunch of free gigs but didn't have anything to sell to your audience, such as CD's, T-shirts, books, DVD's, etc., you really missed out. You may have remembered to tell them about your website, your special offer, or an upcoming show but that's not enough. If you don't have a table set up at your gigs with stuff to sell you are losing money at every gig.

Think of it this way: If you took a free gig and 100 people attended and they really liked you, chances are at least 50 of them would want to buy something to take home. So, if you had a book or CD priced at $10 (depending if you're a speaker or a musician) that's an easy $500. This could definitely pay for your gas, hotels, and food. If you had 200 people in the room, that could have been $1,000. Each and every gig. You're not just selling your merchandise, you're selling the experience. Many people like something to take home to remember the event.

Also, you are not blessing them with something that will benefit them beyond your talk or your performance. They can't even go online afterwards to purchase it (and tell their friends to go online as well!) if you have nothing online to sell.

If you're smacking yourself right about now, take heart. Even though I would NEVER let my bands take a free gig if they didn't have merchandise to sell (aka "merch"), I did a ton of free speaking gigs and drumming events after the accident. I fell for the "Do it for the exposure" ploy. Doing the occasional freebie to get your name out there is fine. Just don't do it consistently.

## The cost of perfectionism and procrastination

There are also intangible costs. These arise from the opportunities you didn't take, the deadlines you missed, the people you didn't connect with, and the things you didn't release out to the world. In your eyes, your project wasn't perfect so you decided to wait. And wait. And wait.

How'd that work for you? Yeah, I thought so. Whatever it was is probably still sitting on a shelf, tucked away in a closet, or sitting on a flash drive somewhere. The cost of not having a plan, or not being organized, and of not having confidence and determination is huge. But that pattern can be reversed. I know because I did it.

My first problem was that I kept assuming that no one would

pay for expensive coaching packages. So, I discounted my prices **and** I added in loads of extras. What I learned was that people who always expect a deal and complain about the price aren't your ideal customers.  I should have remembered this from my tutoring business. Every time I gave the "family and friends" discount, I regretted it. These were the people who did not respect my time and either consistently arrived late, missed sessions (often with no notice!), or conveniently forgot their checkbook. You've got to set boundaries and set your standards higher (and send them a Paypal invoice!). If you're a musician, don't toss free CD's to the crowd.

When I was tutoring, I did have parents who wanted to know why my rates were higher than some of the other tutors. I told them "Because I'm worth it." And then I explained all the things that the student was getting in addition to tutoring:  my vast experience, study skills help, sometimes ADHD tips and dietary suggestions, and I told them the average grade or SAT score jump that my students achieved. Now that I look back, they were getting quite a deal.

**Tip 1**: Don't give away the farm! Those who really want your services, your product, or your talent will be willing to pay a higher price. You are providing them with something of value. YOU ARE WORTH IT! Think of all the time and money you invested in your training, talent, or knowledge. Your pricing goes way beyond the time you spend at the gig or with a client or customer. Some speaking and music gigs are non-negotiable but many are.

**Tip 2:** Let go of perfectionism and stop worrying about what everyone will think. If you're hesitating because you have to learn something new, either learn it or hire someone. That could be the one thing that you need to start earning some decent income.  Just go for it!

Keep in mind that many of the assumptions that you have about yourself are false. Perhaps you have been told them so often, you believed them. All those negative thoughts that are flooding your brain are not serving you and are preventing you from moving forward. And that's exactly what the devil wants. If he can prevent you from realizing your dreams, not only will you feel stuck, empty, and unhappy, you won't be able to do the great things that God intended for you to do. You won't be able to fulfill your unique mission. If you don't believe in the devil, replace the term with dark energy or negative forces. Where there is good, there is evil. Ying and yang.

God wants you to break free. You are His child and unique creation. He would never want you to feel stuck or unworthy. You are valued, you are beautiful, you are talented, and you are loved. You have a purpose and a mission. The trick is to get rid of all the distractions and the things that are holding you back.

**If you've fallen down, you have a choice. You can either stay down or you can choose to get up. #findyourdivinerhythm**

I chose to get up - and keep on rockin'!

**Is it a business or a hobby?**

Ok, so let's say you've forged ahead. You decided to test the waters by doing an open mic night or a show. Maybe you've sold some of your artwork at a fair or art gallery exhibit. Perhaps you've gotten your first client and are jumping for joy. You've snagged a domain name and a website and put up a fan page on Facebook. Does this mean you have a business? No.

You're definitely on your way, which is awesome! However, you need to start setting some financial goals and map out a business and marketing plan if you want to create a viable business model. If you leave caution to the wind and just take things as they come, you'll have a great hobby but it won't be a full-time business. What's the difference?

For me, playing in the church band is a hobby. I don't make any money from it. It's strictly a volunteer position. Drum therapy and drumming events, however, are part of my business. Although I may do a free drum demo or occasional free event, I generally expect to be paid for my services.

Once you start charging for your talent and creativity, then you set the standard and people value your services more. Most creatives, however, are not making enough from their passion. It doesn't matter how much you love it or how much time you're devoting to it. Sooner or later, you have to decide if you're going to take the leap and turn your hobby into a business.

**If it's generating less than $10,000, then it's a hobby.**

Yes, I get that your creativity is a part of your soul and maybe you think using the term *business* is selling out. Maybe you just can't bear to part with your creations or you think that if you consider what you're doing as a business, it will no longer be interesting and fun. I'm going to have to tell you three words: Get over it!

A business does not exist in order to lose money and become a colossal money pit. It exists to sustain you and others and to make a profit. In order to do that, you can't just play around with it. You've got to go *all in*. You're not selling out to "the man". You're saying yes to yourself and your dreams.

**Taking the leap**

So, how and when do you quit your day job? Well, you can't expect to get discovered overnight or have tons of clients lined up right away. You need to have a well thought out exit strategy.

You also need to know how much to charge. This involves doing your research to find out what others in your area are charging. Keep in mind that there is usually room for negotiation, especially for performers.

As I've mentioned, many creatives fall into the trap of accepting little or no pay for "the exposure". While this is ok to do once in a while, this will not sustain you. Eventually, it can also make you resentful. The way to avoid this is to know your worth. State your fee upfront as in "Oh, you need a band to perform for two hours? Well, our fee for that is…." And then be quiet and wait.

Don't start back pedaling and dropping your price before the other person has even said anything! You may have to negotiate a bit or they may say that they need to get back to you. If it's the latter case, make sure you follow up!!

**Often, the person who gets hired is the one who inquired! #findyourdivinerhythm**

Creatives are notorious for dropping the ball. I can't tell you how many bands missed out on opportunities because they never got back to me. These were high-paying festival gigs with a guaranteed payout. I had hand-selected these bands and all I needed to know was "Are you interested and is everyone available that day?" If they didn't get back to me after repeated requests, I chose someone else. I've also had to do this with photographers, printers, and graphic and web designers over the years. It's all about professionalism and customer service.

When you follow up, it's important that you have either a contract (for performers and speakers) or an invoice to send. That way, both parties know what you charge (or what fee you agreed on), what your payment policies are, and what's required. The contracts that I've done are very specific, include contingency plans for inclement weather (and expected levels of payment), equipment and personnel needed, as well as *riders* for food and beverages. I usually discuss all of this verbally with the organizer or venue owner beforehand. I have two different contracts: One for the venue and one for the bands.

I learned the hard way that you need to put everything in writing – and print out a copy of the contract and keep it with you at the event. A casual email or phone call doesn't mean much and won't hold up if there's an issue with payment. You can find free templates for contracts and invoices. Don't be a diva though and ask for ridiculous things like a bowl of M &M's in the dressing room with the green ones taken out.

You're not Van Halen. Be realistic.

**How serious are you?**

What many people do is to initially start their creative business on a part-time basis. They test the waters, see if there is an interest, and then determine how much money they'll need to get started. I've known many people who started working on their business idea at night or on the weekends. Once they started generating business on a regular basis, then they planned their date of departure from their J.O.B. Some have taken off so quickly, it was amazing. It does help to map out a game plan and a budget and we'll do more of that in Chapter 6.

Remember that branding isn't just about what people see or perceive, it's how you feel about yourself. You can't rock your brand if you lack confidence and doubt your abilities to really pull this off. You won't seem convincing.

**It's all about mindset**

Lack of confidence is actually an even bigger problem than lack of startup capital. So is fear of failure. Both can keep you stuck and actually suppress your income for years. What you need to do is to *step out of the cage*! Animals raised in cages or that have been abused are very fearful. Animal rescuers are often amazed that when they try to release the animals and give them freedom, the animals will run back into the cages that have been holding them captive for so long.

They are not used to freedom and the world outside the cage. They want to step out. They can smell the fresh air, they can see the other animals playing, and they can hear their rescuers calling "Come on out, baby! You can do this!" Yes, I sometimes call animals and people "baby". Work with me, here!

After the accident, I ran back into the cage – a lot! I don't want you to make the same mistake. I wasted years doubting myself and my abilities – even though I knew I had all this knowledge and experience. One day, I decided enough's enough. I've spent years pushing other people to realize their potential and their calling.  It was time for me to realize and embrace mine.

Yes, there will be days when it seems like nothing is working or it's just taking too long. The trick is to keep the faith. Know that everyone has bad days (or even seasons) but they don't have to stick with you. They also don't define you. You have to tell yourself that it's time to turn the page and start over. Mistakes are just learning experiences.

**Every day is a new beginning. Time to move on! #findyourdivinerhythm**

When I was struggling, it didn't help to compare myself to other coaches who had a ton of clients and who were making more money than you could possibly imagine. What I didn't know was that they all had stories. They all hit bottom at some point. They managed to pull themselves up, figure out what they wanted to offer and to whom, and they attracted those people.

**How did they do it?**
- They exuded confidence.
- They showed you that they really cared about their clients and their mission.
- They were laser focused on their goals and their mission.
- They acknowledged and claimed their gifts.
- They found who they were intended to serve and regularly contacted them.

- They totally rocked their brand.
- They had multiple income streams.
- THEY STOPPED MAKING EXCUSES AND DECIDED TO GO FOR IT!

**Changing old stories**

In order for your new business or venture to take off, you have to boost your confidence daily. You've got to get all those negative thoughts out of your head and focus on positive outcomes. Many of us have endured cutting remarks from our teachers, parents, siblings, or spouses.

The problem is that, even though we may have dismissed the comments, they can bubble to the surface when things aren't going well. That's a sign that these negative thoughts have lodged themselves so deeply that we have accepted them as fact. Here are some examples:

"You're not smart enough to do that."
"You're just not talented enough."
"You are stupid when it comes to money."

"You can't do that because you're ________ (Fill in the blank with gender, race, nationality, income level, where you live, etc.).

"You'll never amount to anything."

"Your brother/sister is the ____________ (smart one, talented one, athletic one, etc.).

Maybe no one ever said those things to you. Maybe you just put all of that on yourself. Maybe the only one who feels you're a failure is you. Again, we have to go back to some spiritual reasoning here.

If there is a crack in your spiritual core, either recent or from way back when, that is all that is needed for negativity and darkness to creep in. What better way to prevent bright and creative people from making a significant contribution to the world than to whisper lies in their ears that will make them give up?

That's not God talking, that's for sure! He wants you to succeed and thrive, not struggle and suffer. There is no reason why you can't use your gifts and be successful. You don't have to be a martyr and work for next to nothing. You also don't have to allow your past to dictate your future!

Besides, the more money you make, the more money you can actually donate to worthy causes, your church's ministries, or to further your own ministries. Once I realized that I was not only cheating myself and my family by not making enough money but I was cheating a whole lot of causes I could have supported, my perspective changed. I also began to think of all the clients I could have been helping instead of holding back and hiding my gifts.

In fact, let's take another look at the message I heard when I packed up and left home at 16. I later learned it was the beginning of Jeremiah 29:11.

*"For I know the plans I have for you," declares the Lord, "plans to prosper you and not to harm you; plans to give you hope and a future."*

**It's time to step out of the cage and fly!**
**#findyourdivinerhythm**

# Chapter 5
## Backstage Pass: Finding Your Fans by Being Yourself

You may be wondering why I presented so much background info and startup tips but failed to mention that one burning question that most newbies want to know: Where do I find potential clients or fans?

Let's face it, you can't make any money if no one pays for your products or services or comes to your shows. If you don't have a fan base or a prospect list, it's really hard to start generating any income. I'm not saying it can't be done. I'm just saying that it's harder.

I remember when I signed up for an online coaching program. The coach was very informative and inspiring. I took all the information in but then thought: "Well, that's great but where the heck am I going to find clients?" He must have gotten that question thousands of times because he made a video in which he exclaimed: "That's not the right question."

The right questions were *why* and *what*, which is why I covered those first. Another good question is **who**; not only who your idea clients or fans are but who YOU are.

Many of us define ourselves by **what** we do. In fact, it's often the first question people ask when they meet you at a party or event. Very rarely does anyone say, "So, tell me about yourself." Sometimes this comes up during an interview but the expectation is that you'll start spitting out all your work accomplishments.

You certainly wouldn't say "Well, I like curling up with a good book and a glass of red wine or taking long walks on the beach."

So, if someone asked you "Who are you," what would you say?

The sad part is that most people either haven't given this much thought or they've totally forgotten.

You have to really have a handle on who you are so that you present yourself so well that people want more of what you have. They want to know more about you as well. What they really want is a backstage pass.

Keep in mind that once you become more visible and you put your gifts and talents out there, you need to walk the walk and talk the talk. Have you ever gone to see your favorite band, only to discover that the lead singer is a rude and arrogant jerk who disses his band members or his fans or talks trash about other bands?! That totally ruined it for me. And this was a well-known Christian rock band! Talk about being full of yourself!

At another concert, I was standing right next to the lead singer of another well-known band as he told a young fan "Wait here. I'll be right back." He had to take care of something backstage but made sure he came back to sign an autograph for the kid. He even took the time to talk to him. Now, that's class! He was so genuine. You could just feel it. That said more to me that night than his performance.

The version of you that people see should be consistent across the board. That means both in-person and online.

**People want to know the person behind the brand. #findyourdivinerhythm**

## *Take 5!*

Who are you?  Write down a list of descriptive adjectives and attributes and put them in a sentence. You can string together as many as you like. Just make sure you keep them factual and positive! You can write your sentence here:

I'm a....

_______________________________________________

_______________________________________________

_______________________________________________

_______________________________________________

_______________________________________________

Usually, people leave out the one word that is the most important. It's the thing that other people see but you don't. And it's always something very good.

### Behind the curtain

Most people who are just starting out tend to play it really safe. Whether they're on stage, at a vendor fair, writing newsletters or blogs, or doing videos or social media, they generally keep their cards very close to their vests. Everything is very generic and basic and they don't share anything personal.

It's like a keyboard or guitar player who plays but doesn't turn the volume up very high because he is afraid of making mistakes. "Everyone might hear me!" Well yeah, that's the whole point of plugging in, isn't it?

Many creatives and solopreneurs have a problem with visibility. They're not sure that they want to put themselves out there for the entire world to see, so they hold back. This is very evident when I look on people's websites or social media pages. People who are holding back will have something missing: Their photo.

Instead of using a photo, some people use an image, their dog or cat, or their kids or grandkids. Worse yet, they'll leave off the photo altogether! It's difficult to connect with people and get to know them when all you see is an avatar, the Facebook or LinkedIn head, or the Twitter egg!

Another problem is that of very amateurish or bad photos. This is just unprofessional and won't help your brand.

## How to rock your photo

If you have the funds or you have a photographer friend whom you can barter with, I'd say go with a professional photo. You need to find the right type of photographer though. A photographer who is used to doing baby or pet shots might not be able to capture the type of photo you need. You want someone who can bring out your personality, so that your photo doesn't look like an employee ID or a driver's license photo.

Definitely go for a few headshots that are from your shoulders up. You may also want to have a few action shots and some full-length shots. You can use the headshots for your social media profile photo or your one-sheet for speaking engagements or publicity. You can put the others on your website or use them on brochures, posters, or other promotional materials.

As far as outfits, you should stick with solid colors or small prints. The colors you choose can match your website or logo colors or can be the colors that work for your complexion. If you have pale skin or blonde hair, stay away from white, yellow, and beige. If you're in a band, make sure that everyone coordinates their outfits beforehand, so that it doesn't look like a mess of mixed genres.

An example of this would be if one guy decided to go with a plaid, flannel shirt while everyone else in the band showed up with an edgy rock star look with black shirts and pants. Don't be **that** guy! Now, you don't need to all wear the same outfit. Just make sure that the colors or patterns don't clash. If you have absolutely no fashion sense, find someone who does.

If money is an issue, you can just have a friend or relative take your photo, if they have a good camera and some skills. Make sure the background looks cool and isn't lame. I've seen too many shots of people:

- In their kitchen
- In front of steps or a staircase (usually with plenty of glare!)
- In their living room
- In front of their garage

And, of course, the unbelievably unoriginal *band on the railroad track photo*. I guess they think that no one has **ever** thought of that! Unfortunately, everyone has.

Make sure there isn't something else in the shot like a child, pet, someone's hand or foot, etc. You can try to crop stuff out but sometimes it just looks weird. Don't go for a fake background either that just screams Walmart® or Sears® photo center. If you're a solopreneur or a creative and are short on funds, you may be able to get away with a temporary shot using your phone if your phone has enough pixels and the lighting is good.

Your smile and pose should look natural, especially for a headshot. If you're doing a photo shoot, you can have more fun though. Decide what you want the photo to covey and what you want people to think when they see it. Pick one or two words.

With my educational services business, I chose a photo of me that looked friendly, sincere, and "teacher-ish". For the coaching and music business, I wanted some shots that evoked more attitude and fun. These photos can also influence the type of copy you write for your website or promotional materials.

**Making your mess your message**

Another sign of holding back and not being yourself is when you never tell your story. It never appears in your songs, your artwork, your books or articles, your interviews, or your blog posts.

Maybe you're embarrassed by it or just don't want anyone to know. "What will they think of me?" I remember thinking. I thought that telling my story would be professional suicide.

I began to realize that many of the things that I was posting or writing could have been written by anyone. I really wasn't saying anything terribly new and it sounded like a lot of the other coaches out there. Sure, I was giving out a ton of free tips but I wasn't feeling like there was much connection.

It wasn't until I did a newsletter entitled "Are you faking it?" that I began to open up. In it, I revealed my struggles with chronic pain and later, depression. People had no idea that I was wearing Ace® bandages and Icy Hot® patches under my clothes and was in constant pain. They certainly didn't know about the depression. I wrote: "De-nile is a long river in Egypt. And I'm the queen of denial! How about you?"

People began commenting back. It may have been too much information for some people but those who had experienced these issues knew exactly what I was talking about. I made sure that I kept it very encouraging but I wanted people to know that I'm human. I also wanted them to know that they don't have to struggle.

And that's why you were given your story. Yes, it seemed like a mess at the time but your job is to make your *mess* your message. Share your story from the stage or in your writing or artwork. Let people know you're human. Maybe you messed up. Maybe you went through something that was awful. Don't bury it. Talk about it. It will help others heal and it will help you heal as well. No, you don't have to spill your guts all the time but even just alluding to your journey can help.

Maybe it's not something that happened to you but that happened to someone whom you know and love. I know of several people who have written songs or books based on something a family member or friend is dealing with. It affected them deeply and they wanted to raise awareness. Others chose their business or career path because of what their loved one experienced. It's all part of the ripple effect and it can reverberate out and touch more lives than you can imagine.

The famous percussionist Sheila E broke more than 50 years of silence when she recently revealed in her autobiography that she was sexually abused at a very young age. She now has a nonprofit that brings music and music instruction to kids who were abused and neglected. She made her *mess* her message.

Not only has she raised awareness to help kids and teens but she is reaching millions of adults who have kept a similar secret. I just finished reading this inspiring book and I have to say that it brought me more clarity about my own journey than some of the many business books I've read.

Did something happen to you that you're still holding onto? Can you use that experience to evoke change? Stop hiding behind the curtain. Get up and do something! You never know who you can help.

**Who are you serving?**

Now that you've peeled back the curtain a bit and know who you are, you need to figure out who you are trying to reach. Many people think they need to reach everyone with their product, their service, or their talent. They don't have a well-defined personal brand or mission and they definitely don't have a well-defined target market.

So, they try anything and everything to get people's attention. This is called *the spaghetti approach.* You throw everything against the wall to see what sticks. That's not a very good way to tell if pasta is done and it's certainly not a good marketing or business strategy!

Believe it or not, the more you narrow your target market or your audience, the easier it is to find and attract people. It also saves you time and money. Instead of spamming the entire world, why not take some time to figure out:

- ❖ Who is your ideal fan or client?
- ❖ What's his or her age bracket?
- ❖ Is he or she single, married, divorced, still in school?
- ❖ What social media platforms does he or she use?
- ❖ What type of music does he or she listen to?
- ❖ Where does he or she shop?
- ❖ What's his or her income level?
- ❖ What does this person do for entertainment?
- ❖ Does he or she have any hobbies?
- ❖ What types of books does this person read?
- ❖ What kind of car does he or she drive?

- ❖ What is important to this person in their buying experience? What does he or she value?
- ❖ What's this person's price threshold? How much is he or she willing to pay for what you have to offer?
- ❖ How does this person get his or her information and what influences his or her spending? Ads, friends, social media, info on websites, etc.
- ❖ What types of things would he or she like to see offered?

Before you get too overwhelmed, just remember that the first four are the most important. If you're a musician, you certainly want to know what types of bands your fans listen to. All of this information can be discovered by doing some research. Some of it can be found just by lurking on sites or in groups on social media. Services like Spotify tell people what their Facebook friends are listening to, so it can be pretty obvious. Facebook ads also tell you who likes what. I personally find Facebook ads annoying, so I block them. I can still see sponsored posts, however.

You can also send out an email survey, using a free survey tool like Survey Monkey. You can also just call ten people or so and interview them. I didn't get much of a response from surveys but the calls were revealing. Some of the questions may not have much bearing for you or seem too personal, so it's up to you what you include.

**Getting social!**

Explaining the ins and outs of social media marketing and SEO (search engine optimization) would be a book in itself. It also blows most people's circuits! The rules, trends, and algorithms change frequently, so it can be very confusing.

However, you need to be familiar with the different social media platforms, what they're used for, and how to use them. Knowing your target market is pivotal in determining what (if any) social media platforms you should be using.

As of this writing, you have the choice of Facebook, Twitter, LinkedIn, Google+, Instagram, Pintrest, Snapchat, and several new upstarts. I use the first four and may add Instagram and Pintrest, since they're so visual. I'm getting tired of Facebook limiting who sees your posts as a squeeze play to get people to pay for ads, so I'm glad we have other options. I use a free scheduling service called Hootsuite and I schedule my tweets and posts for all my social media accounts in one fell swoop. This takes me about 20 minutes each day. Twitter requires more activity than the others, so keep that in mind.

Many businesses and bands have a fan page on Facebook. Bands also may have a page on Reverbnation and Bandcamp. Artists and photographers should be on Pinterest and Instagram but make sure you watermark your work. Google+ would be good as well. Few creatives really do much on LinkedIn, since it's not the best platform for them but it does have the highest income level, so you never know. The trick is to stay active on these sites and don't let them go dormant.

When people first start out with social media, newsletters, or blog posts, they generally don't know what to write about. As a result, their content sounds like one giant Infomercial to get people to buy their stuff, come to their show, or sign up for their program. What they don't realize is that they're basically screaming at people, instead of talking and interacting with them. I've seen well-known bands say nothing but BUY OUR CD! It makes you just want to unfollow them. It's boring and it's annoying. Again, it's not about you. It's about your audience.

**What works**: People who keep it real! They mix things up and keep it interesting. Pictures get far more likes and views than just about anything. These can include encouraging or inspirational memes (that either you've made or you're sharing) and photos (especially of you doing what you do best: on tour, on stage, on the road, at a vendor fair, at a speaking gig, painting, sculpting, etc.).

Short videos are work well. Facebook just changed their algorithms so that videos now rank higher than photos. It's tough to keep up with all this but it pays to know your audience and what they like. How do you do this? Check to see which tweets and posts get the most likes and the most comments. It's not always the ones you would think!

To improve engagement, you can try the following:

- ❖ Ask a question.
- ❖ Take a poll and have them vote on their favorite tune, painting, design, book title, etc.
- ❖ Do a contest or giveaway. First person who answers a question correctly wins, etc.
- ❖ Post interesting or thought-provoking pictures or comments.

**What doesn't work:**

- ❖ Long Facebook posts.

- ❖ Long blog posts (500 words is the max for most readers.)

- ❖ Blog posts with few or no photos, no breaks between paragraphs, no subtitles. Blogs need to be "scanable" so people can scroll quickly.

- ❖ Lots of text on your website and not many pictures.

- ❖ Tweets or posts with only a link. No one will click these, since it looks like spam.

- ❖ Long, boring newsletters.

- ❖ Headlines that aren't catchy or interesting in some way. No one will open your email or read your blog post, trust me.

- ❖ Tweets and posts that are too pushy. Following the 80/20 rule is key! 80% of your posts and tweets should be informational. Only 20% should be about selling something.

- ❖ Videos that are too long or boring. Ditch the monotone voice and be animated! Informational videos should be 3 minutes or less. A music video can be longer but people may not watch the whole thing.

Remember, social media is supposed to be social! That means there should be interaction. Keep in mind that people are bombarded with information on an hourly basis. They need calls to action (*CTA's*) so that they know what you want them to do. I know it sounds ridiculous but you actually have to tell them to *click here* or *feel free to leave a comment below* (on a blog post or video).

It's also a good idea to respond to people's comments, posts, tweets, and mentions (Twitter), or tags (Facebook). Make sure you answer questions and handle any complaints promptly.

**Keeping the beat**

The trick is **consistency**! You're trying to create a steady beat so that people can follow along. Just like a song, once you start on social media, you have to keep going. You can't just throw something out there and then stop and pick up a month later. People will lose interest and forget about you.

You have to set a schedule and stick to it. The way to do this is by deciding what your goals are for the month. If it's to raise awareness of your band or your brand, that's easy. Just mix up your "all about me" posts with things that your peeps are interested in. Sometimes I add articles from other sources that deal with issues that resonate with my target market. These often get the most shares or retweets! This tells me that I need to write a blog post about this topic or focus on it more.

Add people to your social media tribe! Make sure you connect with not only potential clients or fans but with key influencers as well. These are people who have a ton of followers. One caveat though: Don't just add people for the sake of adding them. They have to be a good match. I get requests from companies all the time. Some are following me on Twitter. The problem is that I'm definitely not their target market. They're just spamming everyone. Again, this is annoying.

Once you start to gain visibility and traction, people will actually help spread the word for you. If they like what you're sharing, they'll start liking, sharing, re-tweeting, etc. You can be a little pushy and ask people: "Please share" or "Please RT" (retweet); just don't do this all the time because it makes you sound too pushy. If something's really good and resonates with people, they'll share it automatically. It's a good idea to put social media links and share buttons on your newsletter and blog posts as well, if you're doing these.

If you find social media way too overwhelming, here's a tip: **Find someone to do it for you!** This could be one of your kids, a college intern, or you could hire a virtual assistant or social media person.

You can't ignore the fact that millions of people are checking their phones and social media on a constant basis. If you don't have an online presence, you are missing out. Also, if you have something to sell and you haven't either set up a shopping cart feature on your website or have a link to another site where your items can be purchased, you're **really** missing out.

## *Take 5!*

Determine which social media platforms would be a good fit for you, based on your industry and your target market. Pick 1 or 2 to start with. Set up your profile and add your profile photo as well. Then, start adding people and write your first tweet or post!

## Other places to find your target market

If you find that social media is way too overwhelming, there are some old school techniques that still work. Attending networking events or MeetUps are great ways to let people know who you are and what you're all about.

You can also attend seminars, conferences, and special events. These are great places to meet people in your industry, key connectors, and also to gain visibility. You may also learn some new tips and tricks! Yes, these cost money but keep in mind that it's considered training, which is a business expense and can be written off your taxes. There are many things that you can write off that you probably aren't even aware of. Memberships to groups and organizations that can further your business or career can be written off as well.

The problem with many creatives is that they don't mingle enough. They stay in their studio or do a show and leave. By not attending arts council meetings and music conventions and not mingling, they miss out on gaining valuable contacts and insight. The same applies to shows and  exhibits. It doesn't even have to be your show or exhibit. Find people you want to connect with and start chatting them up and exchanging contact info.

Keep your business cards with you at all times. If you're an author or musician, keep extra copies of your book or CD with you as well. If you're an introvert, you're going to have to push yourself outside of your comfort zone. As a former introvert, I know this can be done.

Don't think of this as a competition or try to one-up people when you go to these events. When people support one another, everyone benefits. It's a win/win. Yes, some artists and musicians are amazingly supportive, which is great!

However, being a Negative Nellie or criticizing someone else's work isn't good for the spirit or the soul. It's also not good for your career. Imagine if you joined forces and did an event or a show together? Then, you'd share your fan bases and spread the love. I've put bands together in shows for this reason. They had a similar sound and I knew they'd gain fans. It worked every time.

## *Take 5!*

Research different groups and organizations in your area and see if they have any upcoming meetings in the near future. Plan to attend at least one to see if it's a good fit. You can check online ones as well, but meeting in-person has some distinct advantages.

The more you network and help others out, the more people will help you. You don't have to go it alone. Get to know other people and let them get to know you.

**Building your list**

Other ways to build your fan base or prospect list is to get them onto your mailing list. There are two ways to do this:

1) Bring a pad or clipboard with sign-up sheets to shows, exhibits, or speaking engagements.

2) Have a free offer on the main page of your website or on a *landing page* or *squeeze page*. The last two examples are pages you can set up specifically for a special offer or program.

No matter what page you place your freebie, you'll need to set up an opt-in box where people can enter their names and contact info. You, in turn, now have their name on your mailing list. Please be upfront, however, and let them know that this will place them on your mailing list. Indicate that the info will not be sold or shared in any way, so that they feel more comfortable. You can either put the box to the side of the page or make it a pop-up. Pop-ups are annoying but work well.

In order to have this run smoothly, you can sync the opt-in box with a newsletter service like Mailchimp (which is free), or AWeber, Constant Contact, or Infusionsoft (which charge a monthly fee). As soon as someone signs up, you'll be notified and that person will automatically be on your list.

It helps to have something of value to give out with catchy wording. You can switch things out and offer something else, if it seems like no one is signing up. Examples of freebies would be a checklist, article, guide, E-book, or free music download. I've done a couple of mini E-books. I use social media to regularly promote my freebies, blog, videos, and newsletter to gain more subscribers.

**Keeping it real!**

For many people, it's really hard to be open and vulnerable. It's can also be hard to be yourself, if you're always second-guessing yourself or trying to be what you think everyone wants you to be. This tripped me up for such a long time. In fact, it's one of the reasons it took me much longer than anticipated to write this book.

I've been writing business tips for so long and included them in blog posts, newsletters, and videos on my YouTube channel. That's what many people expected this book to be. I was advised to keep my story out of it. That just didn't feel right. I wrestled with this for weeks. Finally, I backed away from my laptop for a while.

During this time, many people kept trying to stuff me back into the "business coach box", explaining that that's what someone with an MBA should do. I would try to tell them that I needed to keep drumming but they'd look at me like I was nuts.  It was like I was revisiting the "You can't be creative **and** smart" argument all over again and I was being forced to choose.

It doesn't help that there are so many dumb drummer jokes out there like:

Q: "What did the drummer get on his IQ test?"
A: "Drool!"

When I read Sheila E's book, I realized what the problem was. I have to drum. It's no longer an option. In order to maintain balance and my sanity, I can't give up drumming. Those who were perceptive knew this and picked up on it. They didn't have to see me drumming to get it. They could hear my voice change when I talked about drumming, even if we were just on the phone. These were people I barely knew. Some I met in Facebook and LinkedIn groups and we decided that we needed to connect.

These were my *sisters from another Mister*. Once you meet kindred spirits like this, you wonder if you were twins separated from birth! They appeared at just the right time with the right message: "Don't give up the drumming. Keep going!" Some confirmed that I'm a healer. This freaked me out at first but when you hear it time and time again, you take notice. God can send you the right people at the right time.

Know that many people will try to deter you. They will criticize you and put you down for going after your dream. In many cases, it's because you are doing something that they're not. Maybe they just don't get it. Or maybe they're just jealous. However, if you know in your heart of hearts that you need to use whatever talent it is you have, **then you need to do it**! You will never feel complete if you don't. So here's a tip:

When people begin to give you advice that you're sick and tired of hearing, insert an index finger in each of your ears and say: "La, la, la – not listening!" And tell them that there is this white chick in her mid-'50's who decided that all she wanted to do was drum – and she did!

Then, apologize to God or the Universe for doubting the Divine plan. Faith and fear cannot co-exist. If you have fear, this is an indication that you lack faith. You need to trust that the plan will unfold – and let go. Keep visualizing your dream and remember God's promises.

**It's time to be the real you! #findyourdivinerhythm**

I will now give you something that you may have been denying yourself: Permission. You have my permission to be yourself and do what it is your heart is telling you to do. The time for holding back is over. It's time to come out of the cocoon and fly!

# Chapter 6
## Keeping the Beat: Creating Momentum and Staying Power

## Time Management and Goal-Setting

Creative and talented types can bless this world in so many ways. They are the innovators, the creators, and the visionaries. They are also the most likely to get distracted and thrown off course. In order for you to stay on track and turn your dreams into reality, you need to get a handle on time management and goal-setting.

It's tough to focus on just one thing at a time when you have 1,000 thoughts in your head at any given moment. Technology and social media have made focusing and time management even more difficult. I once wrote a blog post about how technological advances and social media have actually rewired our brains, creating ADHD traits in just about everyone.

The trick is to train yourself to focus on just ONE thing at a time. Yes, I know that may seem impossible but, if you're highly distractible, it's the only way you'll get anything done.

Every time your phone buzzes or you see an email pop up on your computer, you've lost focus. It's really hard to get back into the zone. If you make the mistake of stopping what you're doing to check that email or Facebook message, it can take your brain up to 15 minutes to get back on track. That's a lot of wasted time each day!

If you find yourself often saying "What was I doing again?" then you are probably not being as productive as you could be. Put your phone on vibrate or stick it in a drawer if you have to. You may need to close your office door or use earbuds.

## *Take 5!*

1) Does it seem like the day goes by and you haven't completed anything? Want to know where your time goes? Try writing out **every single thing** you do in a given day. Keep a log for one day and write down what you're doing and the time it takes. Include meals and breaks.

This not only gives you an idea of how long different tasks are taking you to complete, but it lets you see exactly what your time suckers are. For me, it was social media. I'd go on to post something and then get sucked in by different articles and stories. I thought I was only spending about 30 minutes but it was actually more like 90 minutes to two hours! That's a lot of wasted time!

Keep a pad next to your computer and jot everything down. This exercise tends to be a real eye-opener, so brace yourself.

2) Your next mission is to start thinking about your goals and dreams for the next year. Visualize what you want your life to look like. Close your eyes and imagine yourself doing what is it you want to do. What are you wearing, what do you look like, how do you feel, where does the scene take place and what did you do to get there? Here's an example:

*Photo credit: Dori Staehle*

*A year has gone by and I'm now the lead singer in a jazz band. I'm wearing a silver sequined top and black pants and I'm standing on stage in front of a packed house at the Hippodrome in Richmond, Virginia. All the months of writing, recording, and promoting this event have finally paid off! It feels so amazing to be able to share my gifts with others and I'm bursting with joy! The thunderous applause and calls for an encore have convinced me that this is where I belong.*

**Now, it's your turn! Remember to write your story in the present tense and describe what you're doing, how you feel now that you have achieved this goal, and all the other details.**

*A year has gone by and I'm now......*

It seems real when you can visualize it, right? If you can see it, you can do it!! Don't lose sight of that image! That's your big goal!

## Staying in the pocket

The drummer is the time keeper of the band. A drummer who is all over the place and can't seem to keep the beat will throw off the whole band. He'll push the train off the tracks. Once this happens, it's really hard to get things lined up and back in the groove.

However, a drummer who is *in the pocket* has found the groove and knows exactly what the beat and the fills should sound like. He's synched up with the bass player and everything sounds much tighter. The train is definitely on the tracks and it's easy for the rest of the band, and this percussionist, to ride along.

In order for you to find and stay in the groove, you have to have a game plan. Whereas a musician may need to follow the music, you need to follow a budget. Winging it can only take you so far. Just like it's not good for a drummer to have any holes in the pocket, it's not good for you to have money leaking out of any holes in your pockets either!

## *Take 5!*

1) It would be a good idea to start formulating a budget. Figure out **all** of your existing or projected monthly expenses (including the small stuff) and how much income you would need to cover these expenses. You can use a spreadsheet or program, create a Word document, or write it down on paper.

If you're already in business, hopefully you're tracking your expenses, saving your receipts, and doing monthly income and expense reports. Don't forget things like your cell phone bill, insurance, monthly fees and subscriptions, office supplies, etc.

2) Now, consider how much you'd **like** to make. Most people either aren't sure or they say a really low number. This should be a number that is a stretch for you and makes you feel a bit uncomfortable. It might even make you hyperventilate a little bit. Keep in mind that you get what you expect. If you expect to only make $30,000 or less, you will. Ok, **now** what's your number?

3) What do you need to do to hit that level of income? How many items do you need to sell or how many

shows or speaking gigs will bring in your desired amount? Break it down on a monthly and then a weekly basis.

These are your new income goals. Write them down and get ready! You don't need to map out your entire strategy. Just start with the first two steps. If you're thinking: "Ok, but how the heck do I get from here to there?" hang on.

## Mapping Out a Game Plan

You can't get from Point A to Point B without some type of map or plan. You also won't stay on track. Write down your **top three goals** for this year. What do you already have that can make these goals happen and what do you need? Your list might look something like this:

**<u>Goal #1:   Record a Demo or EP</u>**

**<u>Have:</u>**

1) 3-5 solid tunes that the band can play in just a few takes (The fewer the better. Time is money!).

2) Band members who are available and on board.

3) Decent instruments and amps.

4) A drummer who can play to a click track (some studios require this).

## **<u>Need:</u>**

1) Recommendations for local recording studios.

2) Enough money to cover recording, mixing, and mastering, graphic design for the cover art, copyright fees, CD covers, and duplication fees. Total amount will vary depending on the providers.

3) A crowdfunding campaign to cover the expenses in #2.

4) Samples of successful crowd funding campaigns and videos.

5) Distribution platform (s) and accounts (your website with shopping cart feature, i-Tunes, Reverbnation)

6) Identify and locate target market.

7) Lots of marketing and promotion. Hint: Enlist friends to help!

I chose a musical example but the same process applies to just about anything including writing a book, preparing for a gallery exhibit, organizing speaking gigs, launching a new coaching program, creating a product or educational videos or DVD's, designing and selling T-shirts or jewelry, etc. You don't have to do all of this alone.

**Do what you do best and delegate the rest!**
**#findyourdivinerhythm**

Dori Staehle

## The "Heart" of the Matter

To make sure that you're choosing goals that are a good fit, it's a good idea to consider your *core values*. If you've ever had a job that involved procedures or tasks that seemed unsettling or just didn't feel right, this is most likely because your core values did not match your boss's or the organization's values.

When people aren't moving forward or when they're in a job or a business that doesn't feel right, it's usually because they're not aligned with their core values. They also may not be listening to their heart and honoring their gifts. They are usually making choices based on old thought patterns and beliefs.

## *Take 5!*

1) What words would reflect your core values or what's most important to you at this point in your life? Write

those down below. Some examples might be integrity, spirituality, freedom, creativity, achievement, recognition, etc.

_______________________________

_______________________________

_______________________________

_______________________________

_______________________________

_______________________________

_______________________________

*Feel free to write them in any way, in any pattern, and in any color(s) you choose. These would be items that you could also put on a vision board.

2) **Are any of those words included in your top three goals or are they represented in some way**? For example, if your goal was to write a book, creativity would match. Sharing knowledge would fit as well. If so, match them here:


Goal 1 ______________________________________ Core Value(s)




Goal 2 ______________________________________ Core Value(s)




Goal 3 ______________________________________ Core Value(s)

Do you have different core values for each goal? Do you see any repeats? **Circle those**. Does any word stand out as being the most important to you? That could be your word for the year! Keep this word in mind for your photo shoot and watch what happens!

**Prioritize!**

Pick the **one goal** you can start RIGHT NOW and create a timeline. You then set a deadline and work backwards. If you don't give yourself a deadline, you'll keep pushing things off! Which of the three goals is most aligned with your mission and your values **and** will produce income? Which will take you the closest to your big goal?

**Tip**: Use a spreadsheet or chart **and put all tasks and appointments on your calendar.** I prefer Google Calendar because of its scheduling, reminding, and color-coding features. Some people like agendas or planners. You don't need to know all the steps or have every single resource!

**Here is an abridged version of a book writing goal:**

**Goal**: Write a book by _______________________.

**What's needed**: Time to write, people to help with formatting, editing, cover design, setting it up for sale on Amazon and Kindle. Shortened sample chart:

| Activity | Target Date | Comments/Status |
|---|---|---|
| Create outline | 1/31 | |
| Write chapters | 1/31-3/31 | 2 hrs. each day! Stick to schedule! |
| Cover design (front + back) | 4/1 | Find designer on Fiverr |
| Final Proof | 4/15 | |
| Upload to Create Space + Kindle | 4/30 | |

In reality, there are many more steps, as I discovered. However, I focused mainly on finishing steps one and two.

 **You only need to know the first 2 steps for any goal!**
**#findyourdivinerhythm**

195

Again, set your target date for the final result **first**. Then, work backwards up the chart and fill in and revise as you go. What's needed to actually finish? Do you need a coach or accountability partner? I'm going to be honest here. If I didn't have one, you wouldn't be reading this. Even coaches need coaches!

That is why both group and private coaching work so well. It has to be the right type of coaching and you have to commit to putting in the time and doing the work. It's just like trying to lose weight. The pounds don't magically just fall off. You have to actually make the commitment and change a few things!

## Expanding Your Reach

Another thing to consider is your reach. Do you want to serve people locally, regionally, or globally? You may not know just yet or you might want to just start locally. Knowing your reach can help you clarify your marketing, advertising, and networking efforts. You also need to consider your budget and your skill set.

For example, I first started doing private coaching in-person. The way I advertised my services was by attending local networking events, guest speaking, offering workshops, and through social media. Although I am quite active on social media, this did not grow my client base and my speaking opportunities initially.

After the accident, and when I thought I might possibly be stuck with chronic pain for the rest of my life, I figured I'd better learn how to do some of the techie stuff so that I could offer coaching and drumming online. Thanks to my work with the bands, I already knew quite a bit about social media and how to use it. I had no idea how to make a video and upload it to YouTube and I had never even used Skype or Google Hangouts. I did have experience with blogging, so that was a start.

Through trial and error and a few tips gleaned from webinars, I got the hang of all this. I discovered that I really enjoy filming and editing videos and adding music and animated graphics. I then began connecting with people through Facebook and LinkedIn groups, mainly just commenting on each other's posts or mutual interests.

Soon, I received requests to do online radio shows, Google Hangouts, and teleseminars. I also was asked to be a guest blogger and asked others to do the same for me as well. This way, you can cross promote. Your audience reads the post, as does the other person's. You also both post it like crazy on multiple social media platforms. New fans will visit your website and connect with you on social media.

Eventually, I realized that my reach could be much wider than anticipated. I have to admit, this was a bit scary and overwhelming at first. Even though I'm a real ham and I have no problem on stage, I didn't know if I was the right person for the job. It took many months for me to embrace this vision. I finally figured it was time to give it a shot and just get over it already! I began reaching out to people in the music and speaking industries. I didn't know them personally but like they say, nothing ventured, nothing gained.

If they like your mission and what you have to offer, they might actually want to hear more. Don't stalk them, however! Just find casual ways to connect. I've actually filled some opening slots for my bands this way, especially if I wasn't getting anywhere with the venue owner. I've also gotten sponsorships for shows.

One thing I've learned is that you don't always get another shot. If you're offered something or an opportunity presents itself, you have to be able to react quickly! How many stories have you heard when someone was just in the right place at the right time?

**When opportunity knocks, open the door! #findyourdivinerhythm**

It pays to be nice to people, including the sound guy and the staff at a venue or event. They can talk you up to the powers that be and you may be asked back. You also have no idea who they know. If they really like you, they can put in a good word for you or may have ideas for other events.

Also, don't dismiss people who are trying to talk to you. They might be important or they might know someone who can help you. Make sure you always have your business cards with you or extra copies of your books or CD's. If you invite people like a promoter, agent, or someone from the media to your show or event, make sure you put these people on the guest list. You can also go the extra mile by greeting them at the show, thanking them for coming out, and following up with an email.

These things make you stand out.

If you're a speaker or performer, try to always bring your *A-Game*. Don't be discouraged if there are only a few people there. Give them the same performance whether there are two people in the audience or 2,000. If you feel your energy fading, grab a protein bar or some caffeine. Keep your eyes on the prize and remember your *why*. Remember the fact that this is not about you! It's about your audience! It also helps to consider your legacy.

**What's your legacy?**

Have you ever thought about what you want to leave or pass on to the next generation? What do you want to leave for your kids and your grandkids? If you were doing what you loved and were generating a substantial income, what would you do for them? If you don't have kids (and even if you do) who else would you be able to help?

For me, I'd like to pay off our kids' student loans. I would also love to make this a family business. I'd like to set up a center at some point that would help people in transition and combine entrepreneurship and the arts. I also have an international vision that is much bigger.

Once you start feeling confident that you are on the right path and you're fulfilling your mission, big ideas may come to you. They'll probably scare you at first but don't dismiss them. Just like our visualization exercises earlier, if you can see yourself doing these things or if you can picture what it is you want to create, you're halfway there. God will take care of the rest. He will put people in your path that will help further your dream and your mission.

If your ideas don't scare you a little and you don't have butterflies in your stomach from time to time, you're probably not thinking big enough. Playing it safe is easy. It doesn't require a whole lot of faith. If you're not stretching yourself, you're not growing.  Besides…

**Butterflies are a reminder that it's time to take flight! #findyourdivinerhythm**

## *Take 5!*

**What big things would you do and what would you leave? Jot them down here:**

_________________________________________________

_________________________________________________

_________________________________________________

_________________________________________________

_________________________________________________

_________________________________________________

_________________________________________________

_________________________________________________

_________________________________________________

_________________________________________________

_________________________________________________

## Maintaining momentum

Whenever you start a new venture or start chasing your dreams, it is usually followed by loads of excitement and activity. And then reality sets in. You realize that this is a lot more work than you thought and it requires more time or resources that you expected.

However, if you start slacking off, will this take you closer to your goal or your dream? If you start letting things pile up and don't stay on top of phone calls and emails or all those business cards you collected at networking events, it can get very overwhelming.

Bad habits begin to creep in. You start getting sucked into the social media vortex. Maybe you are spending too much time running errands, going to the gym, or doing things for family members. Either way, you're not taking care of business.

Instead of staying on top of things, you are further away from your goal than ever. You're back to freaking out about where the next client or paying gig is going to come from. Fear begins to rear its ugly head again and you begin doubting yourself.

And you're back on the rollercoaster.

## Developing staying power

Unfortunately, this scenario is very common.  I've met many solopreneurs and creatives who have been at it for a number of years but still aren't getting ahead. What happened?

1) They didn't take themselves, their talent, or their business seriously.
2) They didn't have a system or a timeline in place.
3) They never set up their schedule or if they did, they didn't stick to it.
4) They were totally winging it and didn't have a budget, monthly goals, or ways to meet those goals.
5) They had no marketing plan and weren't familiar with branding.
6) They didn't ask for help!

Sooner or later, a decision has to be made. If the dream is to be kept alive, you have to decide to take your head out of the sand and address the issues. You need to do what it takes to start getting crystal clear about what you want and where you are headed. You also need to figure out what you need to do to develop staying power.

With the exception of a few YouTube sensations, overnight success is rare. Even people or bands who seem new to the scene have really been at it for years. It takes consistent effort and activity. The adage "You're only as good as your last hit" rings true in many circumstances. It's great when you land a major client, deal, or gig. The trick is to be able to repeat the process – again and again.

It also helps to assess what worked and what didn't. Keep in mind that you can control some things but not everything. This is where faith comes in. It helps to be flexible and open to change. You need to trust the process.

**Once you have faith, you can replace worry with wonder. #findyourdivinerhythm**

You'll begin to meet the right people at the right time and opportunities will seem to come out of the nowhere. Actually, it's really because you were in the right frame of mind, your confidence was growing, and you had the faith and expectation that things would work out.

**Tip:** Make sure that you have a solid organizational system and a team in place so that when things really begin to take off, you're ready.

## The importance of multiple income streams

In order to increase your income, you need to be careful not to put all your eggs in one basket. You have to be open to creating other opportunities for yourself. One way to do this is by creating multiple income streams.

## Teaching and recording

For musicians, this means that you might need to consider doing some teaching or recording during the day. Yes, this means that you need to actively pursue clients but this is easier than you may think. However, if you can line up a steady stream **and** make them prepay for a block of lessons or studio time, you just filled your calendar and your bank account. You can even teach lessons online.

The trick is to continue your marketing and advertising efforts so that you can add clients as needed. Some students won't be dedicated and they will either quit or have to miss a lesson. You need to be able to cover this lost income with other students or other activities. Artists, dancers, writers, and photographers can also teach as well. No, you don't need a teaching degree or a Ph.D. You just need to write out a lesson plan beforehand. You don't need a full year's worth. Just write out a few lessons and add as you go.

Keep your records separate for each student, so you can remember what you did the last time, if they're paid up or not, and their contact info. There are programs and apps for this or you can create your own system.

**Speaking**

Another way you can produce income is by doing workshops, retreats, and guest speaking gigs. I did not set out to be a speaker. I realized that there was a demand for the knowledge I had and the educational techniques I developed. I began crafting talks and pitched them to local homeschooling conferences and events. It was a great way to share the information with a whole room of people, instead of just repeating it over and over again to private clients.

Later, I organized and booked my own two-hour workshops. This is the harder route, since you have to provide the audience and you may have to pay to rent the room. The cost of refreshments and any handouts or materials also comes out of your own pocket. All of this is tax deductible but you have to be ok with the fact that you may not cover your expenses and you may lose money. Most of these were low-cost and very affordable.

There are professional speaking organizations and certification programs, if you'd like to go this route. There are huge networks and opportunities for those who are affiliated with organizations like the *National Speakers Association* but you have to have talks that are a good fit. Many of the clients are corporations. You also have to be an experienced speaker with a considerable number of talks under your belt. In addition, you will be reviewed and evaluated by the speaking organization to make sure that your talks are professional and engaging. It would be a good idea to visit a local chapter of the *Toastmaster's* organization to get your feet wet. This organization helps you get started and provides feedback.

For those who are just starting out, there are plenty of small, local organizations that seek speakers on various topics on a regular basis. If you have an area of expertise and a lively or pleasant personality, you can be a speaker. It's a great way to expand your reach and your brand.

Many local organizations expect you to speak for free. This is why it's a great idea to have something to sell at your talks or a program or offering you can pitch. Be sure to bring a sign-up sheet, a pen, and a clipboard so that you can obtain their names for your mailing list. It helps to pass it around or let them know where it is.

**Information products and membership sites**

Other ideas include packaging and selling your expertise. You can record your talks, do DVD's, or just have written materials like a book, E-book, or articles. You can also do online training via webinars, teleseminars, video, or Google Hangouts (aka HOA's, or Hangouts on Air). Some solo artists and bands host private HOA's and charge for their online concert. They broadcast from home and might have a moderator help them out.

Some coaches and music teachers have membership sites. These are paid programs. Participants are provided training videos or handouts in return. Clients are given a special access code or the materials may be sent directly.

**House parties**

Hosting a workshop (or *house party* for musicians) in someone's home is another great way to make money. I've done this before. The host or hostess provides the drinks and snacks and invites people for you. You make it worth the host's while by providing something of value in return. You can set up an invitation on Eventbrite.com and charge for tickets. You then send the link to the host or hostess to promote to their peeps and ask if you can invite your friends as well.

**Creating online systems**

Having a newsletter list and a good number of social media contacts enables you to promote your offerings quickly and effectively. You can also ask others to help promote what you're offering. Don't just splash your stuff on someone's wall, however! Send them a message and the link and ask if they'd mind promoting you.

Many people have set up a system on their website so that people can purchase items from them 24/7. That's called making money when you sleep! It helps to have autoresponders like Mailchimp, A-Weber, Constant Contact, or Infusionsoft. I listed those in order of cost. There are other ways you can set this up yourself, if you have some techie knowledge.

**Licensing deals**

Another great way for musicians and artists to create additional income is through licensing deals. You can license your artwork to be used on other products such as T-shirts, mugs, posters, puzzles, calendars, and greeting cards, for example. Bands and solo artists can license their tunes for commercials, movies, and video games.

It helps to have an agent to represent you and to screen these deals for you. You might also want to have an attorney look over any contracts before you sign on. Not all deals and licensing companies are created equal. I've screened and turned down dozens for my bands and solo artists. If you get a good deal, the residual income can be extremely worthwhile. Companies like the international A&R firm *TAXI* specialize in these types of music deals. Artists like Tift Merritt have made more from licensing deals than from touring.

*Full disclosure:  TAXI has sponsored some of my huge concerts and I am now an affiliate. I do get paid a small fee for recommending them but I would never recommend anything that wasn't legit. TAXI membership includes listings, screening, and free tickets to their yearly music conference in LA. If interested, use my ID#: ST1932 and tell them that Dori sent you!*

**Affiliates, advertisers, sponsorships, and endorsement deals**

Another way to boost your income would be to consider partnering with different organizations and becoming an affiliate. I mentioned my arrangement with TAXI but there is another way to make extra income with affiliates.

If you've noticed ads on people's websites or YouTube channel, they are getting paid per click. There are ways to boost your SEO and your views so that you increase traffic to your website and your YouTube channel. There are people on YouTube who are making from $1,000-$10,000 per month (and more!) from these arrangements. Having a boatload of subscribers can do this for you. Yes, there are people out there who can help you set all that up.

Some performers and speakers have sponsors and endorsement deals. Sponsorships can help cover the costs of one event or show or several. I used to offer different sponsorship levels to the companies that sponsored my Battle of the Bands events, for example. Each level had different perks. This needs to be presented in a formal and very professional way, just like a contract. Sponsors can be local or national businesses or individuals. One perk for a large sponsor is to hang their banner at your show or event, either on stage or at your table. Advertising on your website (with a link) and in print materials is a must.

You can also seek endorsement deals from companies whose products you use. This is very common for musicians. Once you gain exposure, you may want to seek endorsement deals. Keep in mind, they have to see the benefit and be convinced that you have a decent reach. This can happen quickly, so get ready!

**Enlisting support**

Once things start to take off, you may find that you just can't juggle everything and keep all those plates in the air. That's when you need to assess what is sucking up your time and what you need to delegate to others. If you find that you're spending way too much time on administrative tasks, or if you are getting behind on orders or emails, then it may be time to hire someone to help. If you have the funds, you might look into hiring a virtual assistant or *VA* for a few hours a month. They generally charge about $30-$40/hr. They can be in your hometown or anywhere in the world.

If not, you may want to check your local college to see if you can find a student intern. This could be a paid or unpaid internship. Keep in mind that you will need to be able to communicate effectively, provide instructions and possibly some training, and you may need to complete the necessary paperwork so that the student receives college credit.

If you don't have the funds to pay for a student intern, find other ways to compensate them to show your appreciation. This could be in the form of gift cards, concert tickets, or other perks. If they're living in the dorms, they're probably sick of the food in the dining hall, so homemade meals or coupons to local restaurants are always a safe bet.

If you have teens at home, enlist their services! Have them take care of all those business cards you have hanging around. Have them enter them into your database for you and categorize them. They can probably set up your Facebook fan page and any other social media account (and teach you how to use it). They can also do spreadsheets for you if you want to set up a call list or map out a timeline. If you need a presentation, I'm sure they can set it up for you on Powerpoint.

Paying them $10 an hour would be worth it. If your hourly rate is $100-$200 an hour, you shouldn't be doing $10-$15/hr. activities.

## *Take 5!*

**Self-assessment**

1) What are you not keeping up with? Make a list.
2) If you had a better system, could you take care of these things yourself?
3) Is there anything that's not in your skill set that someone else should be doing? Be honest!
4) Who do you know who could help you with these tasks or where will you go to find them?
5) When do you plan to take care of this? Give yourself a deadline.

Time to take a breath! I've thrown lots of ideas at you but don't worry! You don't need to do a 6-page business plan or worry about applying for a small business loan. In fact, contrary to popular belief, lack of capital is not what causes entrepreneurs to fail. It's lack of confidence.

You have to stand firm, hold onto your dream, and believe not that what you want **can** happen but that it **will** happen. It's building enough resolve so that you don't buckle when things don't go exactly the way you expected or when the naysayers start swarming. It helps to be flexible and go with the flow. Once I recovered from my injuries, I realized that I didn't have to restrict my movements anymore. I had to recondition my brain and my body. I was finally free. And you can be too!

There comes a point when your passion becomes so strong that there is no stopping you. You don't take "No" for an answer and you JUST KEEP GOING! But you have to feel it. If you don't feel excitement and passion for your dream, then it may not be the right dream. Or it may not be the right time. And that's ok. It all boils down to this:

**If you really want to do something, you'll find a way to do it. #findyourdivinerhythm**

It helps to have buy-in from friends and family but you may have to sell them on your idea. Many creatives succeeded without any family support of any kind. You can't use that as an excuse. You have to be willing to do what it takes and to jump on opportunities as they come your way.

If you start backpedaling or feel fear creeping in, remind yourself that you can do this! You have the talent and the skills. Feel the fear and do it anyway. You can't hang out backstage forever. Sooner or later, you have to step into the spotlight and grab the mic! It's time for you to rise up and rock YOUR next stage!!

**This is your time! This is your dream! Go for it!! #findyourdivinerhythm**

*D*ivine

*R*hythm

*U*nique

*M*ission

## Conclusion

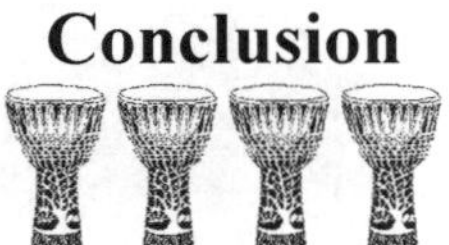

It's never too late to start over. Even if you think you've messed up, you can always get back up and give it a shot. Whenever I thought the deck was stacked against me or felt ready to give up, I remembered those who faced more difficult circumstances, yet they succeeded.

Some of the most successful people have overcome obstacles that you can't even imagine. What makes them different? They didn't quit! They kept the faith and they believed in themselves. They believed that there was more to life than what they were presently experiencing. And they believed that they were created to give something back to the world.

It was more than just lucky breaks. They kept at it and learned what they needed to know to make them stand out in their field. They connected with the right people and asked for help and advice when needed. They also had a game plan and a positive attitude.

I've seen people of all ages start businesses, come up with inventions, or take their talent to the next stage – and generate a solid income! All because they took a chance, had a whole lot of faith, and just said "What the heck?!"

If I can bounce back from adversity and turn a crazy hobby into a viable business, anything is possible! If I can do this, you can too!! Remember:

**Change starts with a decision.  #findyourdivinerhythm**

I hope that this book has given you hope, as well as some ideas on how you can use your talents and creativity to create a business that rocks and a life that you love. Know that I've been praying for you. I know you can do this!

You're never too old to go after your dreams and do what makes your heart sing. You've waited long enough. It's time to rock YOUR next stage!

*May he give you the desire of your heart and make all your plans succeed.* ~ Psalm 20:4

**Interested in private coaching?** I'd love to help you move your dreams forward! You can contact me at dori@rockthenextstage.com.

**Website and social media:**
**www.rockthenextstage.com** (Free weekly newsletter!)
Facebook: www.facebook.com/rockthenextstage
Twitter: @rocknextstage
LinkedIn: www.linkedin.com/in/doristaehlemba
Google+: +DoriStaehle and +RocktheNextStage
Subscribe to my YouTube Channel!
www.youtube.com/user/rockthenextstage

**Booking:**
To book Dori for speaking or for a drumming event:
Email: dori@rockthenextstage.com
Phone: 919-906-7842

*Life's short! It's time to rock what you've got!!*

# *A Special Bonus from Dori*

This book is the start of your journey to understanding what makes you unique, what has been tripping you up, and how you can use your gifts and talents to succeed. I'm sharing my story and plenty of tips to help you move forward and create a solid income.

It took me several years to bounce back and find my rhythm. It also took quite a lot of soul-searching and conversations with God. These conversations became daily journal entries. I am sharing some of these entries in the form of a 30-day affirmations journal which is yours free! It will help you stay focused and encouraged and see the big picture. You can print out a page a day, if you like, or keep it on your computer.

Download your copy here:
*http://www.rockthenextstage.com/divinerhythmjournal*


*Get ready to rock!*

*Dori*

## About the Author

Dori Staehle, MBA is from the Raleigh, NC area and is the Chief Encouragement Officer and Rhythm Maker at *Rock the Next Stage*. She's a motivational and faith-based speaker, business and success coach, drum therapist, and drum healer. Dori's passion is to encourage, empower, and equip creatives so they can move their talent or their business onto the next stage and rock their brand from the inside out.

After she was derailed by a freak accident, Dori found her rhythm and rose up from the ashes. She reconnected with her love of drumming and found ways to help creatives heal, move forward, and start a rockin' business.

Dori started her first business in 1995, while raising and homeschooling her 2 kids who are now grown and gone. Dori is a proud grandmother of a beautiful little grandson and lives in the Raleigh, NC area with her husband Mark, and 2 orange tabbies, Sadie and Simon. In her spare time, Dori plays percussion with the rockin' band at New Horizons Fellowship in Apex, NC.

***Finding Your Divine Rhythm: A Creative's Success Formula*** provides insights and revelations about creative types and the issues they face. It also offers proven strategies that creatives can implement **right now** to start earning a solid income. Dori Staehle, MBA has 20 years of research and experience in the areas of giftedness, ADHD, and creativity, and also has 20 years of experience as an entrepreneur, including 15 in the music business.

*www.rockthenextstage.com/ dori@rockthenextstage.com*
*www.facebook.com/rockthenextstage / Twitter:*
*@rocknextstage/ 919-906-7842*